Foraging in the Pacific Northwest

A Complete Beginners Guide for Identifying, Gathering, and Preparing Edible Wild Plants – Edible Plants Survival Guide

Armand Hansen

the information contained within this document, including, but not limited to, errors, omissions, or inaccuracies.

Icon on the cover designed by freepik from Elaticon

Table of Contents

Click <u>Here</u> for the guide!

Your Free Gift!

As a thank you for choosing this book, we've included this handy guide to the hiking trails of the Pacific Northwest, specially written for foragers, as a free gift for our readers.

In this guide, you'll find:

- An overview of the hiking trails of the Pacific Northwest, and which are the best to forage on

- Important information about the plant life and climate of each trail, to ensure you have the best hiking and foraging experience possible

- Essential safety notes, such as which trails pass through bear country, that every hiker or forager should know

- And so much more!

https://armandhansen.com/your-free-gift/

As you read earlier, I'm going to provide you edible plant profiles that are prevalent in the Pacific Northwest. Colored pictures have been uploaded in the digital guide to help you recognize them.

In case you are reading the hardcopy/paperback edition of this book, then you can just scan the QR code below to obtain a complete full-color look at these plants. Happy foraging and enjoy the book!

Introduction

Fig 1. A forest in the Pacific Northwest. From: Unsplash, by Dave Hoefler, 2018.
https://unsplash.com/photos/rcE3_D-u2NE. Copyright Dave Hoefler/Unsplash, 2018.

In prehistoric times, foraged foods would make up a vast majority of our ancestors' diets. People around the world have continued to rely on foraged foods up until this day. However, today many people in modern American society have forgotten about the bounty that nature offers us, and are missing out on delicious meals prepared with herbs, berries, and mushrooms growing wild all around them!

However, in recent days, interest in foraging has skyrocketed again. Many people are feeling dissatisfied with spending much of their time indoors and are looking for ways to get back outside and get back in touch with nature. Other people may be avid fans of the outdoors already, and want to start taking advantage of the natural resources growing all around them. Still, others are worried that the abundant food supplies in grocery stores won't last forever and want to start looking into ways to feed themselves off the land.

Whatever your reasons, you've come to the right place. With this guide, you'll have everything you need to dive into foraging in the Pacific Northwest, whether you're a resident of Idaho, Oregon, or Washington, or just a visitor to the area! We'll go over some of the most common edible and medicinal plants in the region, and how best to harvest them. We'll also look into some delicious recipes for when you bring home your harvest, as well as ways to preserve your harvests in the form of jams, pickles, and more. Furthermore, we'll be touching on the medicinal uses of foraged plants, as well as some herbal teas you can make to treat minor ailments such as sore throats or constipation.

This manual will also extensively discuss how to keep not only yourself, but the surrounding environment safe when you're out foraging. You'll learn how to navigate unexpected encounters with wildlife, how to determine when it's safe to go out and forage, and what you need to bring with you to be prepared. You'll also learn how to harvest wild plants ethically, to ensure that they continue to grow wild for future generations to enjoy.

From the beautiful Cascade mountains to the stunning coastline, the Pacific Northwest has plenty to offer the prospective forager. With this guide, you can be sure that you're not missing out!

Chapter 1:

Edible Plants of the Pacific Northwest

While it would take thousands of pages to catalogue all of the edible and medicinal plants in the Pacific Northwest, some of the most common varieties are listed here. Never eat a plant if you are not 100% sure what it is, and don't identify plants by comparing pictures: Ensure that they have all of the physical traits listed as well! Beginner foragers are encouraged to seek in-person guidance from a more experienced forager on their first trips.

Plants and Herbs

Agoseris (Agoseris spp.)

Commonly thought of as a weed, the common agoseris flowers are just as edible as dandelions, their close lookalikes.

Identifying Characteristics

Look for agoseris in open places with a lot of sunlight. These hardy plants grow in meadows, on hillsides, sloping areas, and at the base of hills and mountains. The plant resembles dandelions, with thinner stalks and differing flower shapes. Agoseris grows in single plants, with a cluster of leaves at the base and the long-stemmed flower extending from the middle. Agoseris flowers can grow up to 20 inches tall.

Besides the most common yellow variant, there are also orange-flowered agoseris plants, as well as "short-beaked agoseris" (*agoseris glauca*) which grows on prairies. While agoseris leaves are generally long, thin, and resemble stalks of grass, the leaves of these variants are wider, flatter, and oblong in shape.

Edible Parts

The stalks, leaves, and flowers of the agoseris plant are edible raw, and can be added to salads or dried and mixed into teas.

Notes

Dried sap from agoseris stems hardens into an edible, chewy substance that can be made into a natural chewing gum!

Fig 2 Beargrass in bloom. From: Pixabay, by Ellen26, 2016. https://pixabay.com/photos/beargrass-white-flower-wild-flower-1282962/ Copyright Ellen26/Pixabay 2016.

Beargrass (Xerophyllum Tenax)

This common wildflower grows beautifully in open spaces around the Pacific Northwest. Bears often collect this plant to use as bedding in their dens, hence the name.

Identifying Characteristics

These plants are found in full sunlight, at hillsides, forest edges, and clearings. Beargrass does not grow in wet regions and prefers dry, well-drained soil. Beargrass plants grow up to five feet tall. When blooming, their long, green stems are topped with thick clusters of white flowers, with pointed petals and long stalks extending from the centres. Long, thin leaves grow from the base of the stems.

Edible Parts

The edible part of beargrass is the thick rhizome, found at the root of the plant, which resembles a tuber. Before eating, boil or roast the beargrass rhizome as you would with a potato.

Bedstraw (Galium spp.)

Also known as "cleavers," this hardy plant has a number of varieties growing up and down the Pacific Northwest. Bedstraw is a great source of Vitamin C.

Identifying Characteristics

Bedstraw grows around recently-disturbed soil or places inhabited by short, low growing plants. Bedstraw grows in patches or clusters, with bright green, oblong leaves pointed at the ends that grow outwards in rings from the tall stems. The leaves of the plant are covered in small hairs. Depending on the age of the plant, small white flowers with four pointed petals may grow in clusters at the tops of the stems.

Edible Parts

To avoid a bitter taste, harvest small/young bedstraw plants that have not yet fruited. The leaves, stem, and flowers of the bedstraw plant are all edible but tasteless raw. Toss into a stir fry, curry, or soup for best results.

Notes

Bedstraw has mild laxative properties, so limit consumption if this isn't the effect you're looking for!

Fig. 3. Broadleaf plantain. From: Pixabay, by AKuptsova, 2020. https://pixabay.com/photos/plantain-medicinal-

Broadleaf Plantain (Plantago Major)

A common weed and one of several edible plantain species growing throughout America's forests, broadleaf plantain is common throughout the Pacific Northwest and very edible both raw and cooked.

Identifying Characteristics

Broadleaf plantain can grow basically anywhere, but prefers moist and nutrient-rich soil. Look for a plant with long, fibrous roots and leaf-stems, also known as petioles, that can get as long as six inches. These petioles grow outwards from a central point, giving the plant a rosette-like appearance. Young plantain petioles are oval-shaped, smooth, and bright green, while older petioles are darker and pointed towards the ends. Some varieties grow hair on older petioles, while others remain smooth to the touch. Plantain petioles also have distinct veins that run the entire length of the leaves, and in some cases, the petioles will take on a reddish tint near the centre point. The stalks of the plant grow from the center of the rosette and flower between June and September. Flowers take the form of small, pale petals that coat the upper parts of the stalks. Mature plantain stalks are coated with seed capsules carrying up to 30 seeds each.

Edible Parts

Young plantain leaves are edible raw, and are very fresh-
tasting: Perfect for salads. Since the leaves have a fibrous
and chewy texture, they are best shredded into small pieces.
Older leaves can be eaten steamed or otherwise thoroughly
cooked. Plantain seeds can be dried and then crushed into a
flower that can be incorporated into baked goods or used
as a thickener.

Fig. 4. Cattails with cigar-shaped flowerheads. From:
Unsplash, by Denny Muller, 2020.
https://unsplash.com/photos/WVRGWpbn37Y
Copyright Denny Muller/Unsplash 2020.

Cattails (*Typha Latifolia.*)

With hundreds of variants growing across the Americas, including in the Pacific Northwest, this member of the grass family is one of the most common edible plants in the region.

Identifying Characteristics

Look for cattails in areas where the ground is wet, such as marshes and around the edges of ponds. The plants have tall stalks, topped with cigar-shaped or cylindrical brown heads. A thin yellow spike extends from the top of the cattail head. Leaves extend from near the bottoms of the stems, are very long, and stand upright. Cattails can reach between 5 and 10 feet in height.

Edible Parts

Cattails are known for the high starch content in their roots. Starch is the same substance that makes up the bulk of wheat, barley, and other grains, and thus, dried and ground cattail roots can be used to make flour. The cigar-shaped 'flowers' of young cattails can be tossed in oil and roasted, while the young shoots and leaves can be eaten raw, boiled, or steamed.

Native American peoples found many uses for cattails besides food, including using them to make diapers, baskets, and torches.

Chickweed (Stellaria Media)

Chickweed is an invasive weed that was brought to North America with European settlers. While a great annoyance to gardeners, chickweed is one of the easiest wild plants in the Pacific Northwest to find!

Identifying Characteristics

Chickweed grows in cool, damp soil. Leaves are dark green, oblong, arranged in rings around the stalk, and have a stringy texture. The stalk grows only two to four inches off of the ground and is adorned with one distinctive line of hairs running up the entire stem. Something else distinctive about chickweed is how tiny the flowers are, if present at all. The small flowers should have five white petals with deep clefts in the middle ringing a green center and grow at the end of a stalk. On some flowers, these clefts are so deep there appear to be 10 petals.

Edible Parts

Young chickweed leaves are edible raw. However, the above-ground parts of the chickweed plant can be eaten cooked, and this is thought to make it more palatable.

If you find a chickweed plant covered in small hairs, this is the mouse-hair variety: They are still edible, but much less palatable. If you find a similar-looking plant without any hair, leave it alone; it might be a toxic lookalike.

Devil's Club (Oplopanax Horridus)

Despite the frightening name, this plant has a variety of useful medicinal applications!

Identifying Characteristics

Found across the entire Pacific Northwest, Devil's club grows in shaded wet soil near running water. Leaves are bright green, very broad, and shaped like maple leaves. The stem of the plant can grow up to 10 feet tall and is covered in sharp thorns. Stems are topped with clusters of small white flowers in spring and bright red, spherical berries in summer.

Edible Parts

Do not eat Devil's club berries because they are very toxic! However, the stems and roots can be harvested for medicinal purposes. Devil's club roots are often peeled and included in medicinal teas or poultices.

Fig 5. Goldenrod flowers. From Unsplash, by Jeffrey Hamilton, 2019.
https://unsplash.com/photos/JMuJfLVWtN4.
Copyright by Jeffrey Hamilton/Unsplash 2019.

Goldenrod (Solidago spp.)

While goldenrod is considered an invasive weed in some regions, this herb has been traditionally used medicinally for hundreds of years. Though scientific evidence for goldenrod as a medicine is lacking, this common herb is still perfectly safe to eat.

Identifying Characteristics

Goldenrod grows in full sunlight, often in plains, meadows, and at the base of hills and mountains. Look for long, branching stalks growing up from the ground with bright green, oval-shaped leaves placed alternately along the entire lengths. Goldenrod flowers are densely clustered, bright yellow, and grow from both the stalk itself and the upper level of branches.

Edible Parts

While goldenrod flowers can be eaten raw, the whole plant is edible when cooked. Try steaming goldenrod stalks with your favourite seasonings! Goldenrod seeds can be roasted or eaten raw.

Notes

Mullein, another common herb, is often confused for goldenrod, but it's easy to distinguish the two with a little foreknowledge. Mullein flowers are less densely placed, and have four square-shaped yellow petals per flower. Mullein stalks are also unbranched, and grow from circular basal clusters of wide, flat leaves.

Fig: 6. An unripe gooseberry. From: Unsplash, by Friderike, 2020. https://unsplash.com/photos/IyulfxSdgWE Copyright Friderike/Unsplash 2020.

Gooseberries (Ribes spp.)

Identifying Characteristics

Gooseberries prefer moist soil and are often found in the foothills of mountains or other elevated regions. Gooseberries grow on shrubs that are distinctively covered in thorns, including the twigs. Some variants have thorns growing out of berries themselves. The leaves of the gooseberry shrub are bright green, three-sectioned, serrated on the edges, and resemble maple leaves. Before bearing fruit, the gooseberry shrub bears red flowers arranged in a line along the length of the branches. Gooseberries are arranged the same way; red, orange, or yellow in color, and have stems that hang down from the bottom of the berries. As mentioned above, berries are covered in thorns in some variants.

Edible Parts

The taste of gooseberries is described as very tart. Their high pectin content makes them great for jams and jellies, though they can be eaten raw: Be sure to remove the thorns first! Gooseberries are also great when baked into pastries and pies, as the sugar helps mellow out their tart flavor.

Fig: 7. Close up of late-summer horsetail stem and leaves. From: Pixabay, by ArtTower, 2013. https://pixabay.com/photos/horsetail-scouring-rush-plants-123013/ Copyright ArtTower/Pixabay 2013.

Horsetails (Equisetum Arvense)

The medicinal properties of horsetails are well known, and have been for thousands of years. Galen, commonly thought to be one of the fathers of medicine (129-199 AD), wrote extensively about its uses.

Identifying Characteristics

Horsetails have a grass-like appearance, and are made of long, thin stems which reach over three feet in height. Look for them in regions of moist soil, especially high-traffic areas where the soil is likely to have been disturbed. In early springs, horsetail stems are brown and topped with brown cones, which disappears when the plant releases its spores. Later in summer, look for bright green stems with 'joints' that give them the appearance of multiple stems joined together. Leaves are long, tube-shaped, and angled upwards towards the sky. The leaves are arranged in rings around the stems.

Edible Parts

The above-ground parts of horsetail are edible when cooked. Try incorporating it in a stew, stir fry, soup, or curry. Horsetail can also be dried and made into a delicious and medicinal tea.

Fig 8. Huckleberry bush bearing fruit. From: Pixabay, by Goumbik, 2017. https://pixabay.com/photos/hand-berry-nature-bush-natural-2717117/ Copyright Goumbik/Pixabay 2017.

Huckleberry (Vaccinium spp.)

Huckleberries are a beautiful and highly sought-after plant present along the western sides of Washington and Oregon. Prized for their tasty berries, these large shrubs grow primarily in thickly wooded areas.

Identifying Characteristics

Huckleberries grow on shrubs that can reach heights of 10 feet and widths of five feet. The stalks of the plants are generally brown, but keep an eye out for newer plants with bright green stalks.

Huckleberry shrubs flower before bearing fruit. The flowers are pale or light pink, waxy, and take the shape of a cup or bud. The berries are bright red, blue, purplish or back when ripe, and very round, similar in shape to blueberries. The tops of the berries have a distinct ring shape, sometimes with a stem poking out from the centre. Huckleberry plant leaves are elliptical in shape, with a bright, glossy green color that is lighter on the underside.

Edible Parts

The berries of the huckleberry plant are edible raw or cooked. When raw, they have a tart, sour flavour. Huckleberries taste much sweeter when cooked into pies, pastries, and other baked goods.

Notes

In winter, red huckleberry plants lose their distinctive leaves, but may still be bearing fruit. This makes it hard to distinguish red huckleberries from similar-looking inedible species. It's best not to harvest red huckleberries in winter for this reason.

Indian Pipe (Monotropa Uniflora)

Fig 9. An Indian pipe blossom. From: Pixabay, by brosimoff, 2019. https://pixabay.com/photos/ghost-pipes-monotropa-uniflora-plant-5756786/ Copyright brosimoff/Pixabay 2019.

Indian pipe, also traditionally called ghost flower, is known for its striking all-white appearance. Indian pipe is parasitic, and instead of getting nutrients from the soil, draws what it needs from a larger tree or plant.

Identifying Characteristics

Thanks to it's unusual appearance, the Indian pipe plant is hard to miss. In damp, thickly forested regions, look at the base of large, old trees for groups of thick white stalks topped with drooping white flowers. The flowers are tube-shaped, angled towards the ground, and yellow in the centres.

Edible Parts

While snacking on raw Indian pipe won't hurt you, it has a bland to non-existent taste. Steaming or otherwise cooking Indian pipe brings out a bitter vegetable flavor, similar to that of asparagus or brussels sprouts.

Notes

Indian pipe contains glycosides and is poisonous in large quantities. Enjoy in smaller amounts to avoid getting sick, or reserve for medicinal uses (more on this in Chapter 7).

Fig: 10 Mature knotweed blooms. From: Pixabay, by HOerwin56, 2017.
https://pixabay.com/photos/knotweed-shrub-plant-2699120/. Copyright HOerwin56/Pixabay 2017

Knotweed (Polygonum spp.)

Knotweed refers to a group of creeping edible plants found throughout the Pacific Northwest. While it is considered a weed, knotweed actually has a number of edible parts.

Identifying Characteristics

As knotweed grows most easily in drier regions, look for it on sunny plains and around the foothills of mountains. The plant grows in long, thin stalks with creeping rhizome branches that tangle together, resulting in the formation of thickets. Swollen joints or nodes are interspersed along the stems. Leaves are narrow, football-shaped, usually less than an inch long, and placed alternately along the stem. Flowers are greenish, grow in clusters on branching stems, and petals can be whitish or pinkish when mature. Small fruits bearing one seed each are found in the centre of the flowers. Seeds are brown and egg-shaped.

Edible Parts

Knotweed seeds can be eaten raw, roasted, or pounded into meal and used to thicken sauces or cooked dishes. The rest of the plant can be eaten if cooked. Try tossing it into a stew or curry for best results.

Fig 11. Fiddleheads ready for harvest. From: Pixabay, by ulleo, 2021. https://pixabay.com/photos/fern-fiddlehead-plant-spring-6258134/ Copyright: Pixabay/ulleo 2021.

Lady Fern Fiddleheads (Athyrim Filix-Femina)

Fiddleheads are a type of fern found throughout North America, known for their distinctive curled shape that resembles the top of a violin. While there are a number of variants, the most common variety in the Pacific Northwest is the lady fern fiddlehead.

Identifying Characteristics

Look for lady fern fiddleheads in shady patches of forest, in regions where the soil is moist. Lady fern fiddleheads have two to seven fronds and can reach two to three feet in height. The stalk of each frond has a distinctive groove running down the backs and is topped with a spiral-shaped rosette. Lady fern fiddleheads are bright green in color, but may be decorated with some brown, mushy foliage.

Edible Parts

The spiral-shaped head of the lady fern fiddlehead is edible when cooked. Try fiddleheads steamed, sauteed, or added to stews, soups, and curries. Do not eat fiddleheads raw, and ensure that any dead brown foliage is washed off before eating. Fiddleheads also taste good pickled with garlic.

Lady fern fiddleheads are known to grow near horsetails: If you spot one, the other may not be far away!

Fig 12. Miner's lettuce in bloom. From: Pixabay, by WikimediaImages, 2014.
https://pixabay.com/photos/beargrass-white-flower-wild-flower-1282962/ Copyright by WikimediaImages/Pixabay, 2014.

Miner's Lettuce (Montia Perforliata)

While sometimes elusive, miner's lettuce is perfectly edible and known for its refreshing taste.

Identifying Characteristics

Miner's lettuce grows in shady regions, especially at the base of trees or hills. Moist soil is a must for this plant. Look for clusters of thin, green stems. Younger miner's lettuce stems may be dark red at the base and fade to green towards the tops. The stems are topped with a single oblong, cup-like leaf, and sometimes also small white flowers or buds. Some foragers report that miner's lettuce often grows near bedstraw.

Edible Parts

The entire plant is edible raw or cooked. Miner's lettuce can be enjoyed in salads, in soups or stews, or baked into baked goods.

Fig 13. White mulberries. From: Pixabay, by byrev, 2013. https://pixabay.com/photos/alba-morus-mulberry-white-fruit-88456/ Copyright byrev/Pixabay 2013.

Mulberry (Moura spp.)

Best known from the famous nursery rhyme (all around the mulberry bush…), mulberries are a delicious fixture of the Pacific Northwest. Similar in appearance to raspberries, these sweet berries are an essential stop on any berry-picking expedition.

Identifying Characteristics

Mulberries grow on large, woody bushes, which have thin branches expressing flat leaves with serrated edges. The berries, like raspberries, have a clustered shape (this is known as a compound berry). Ripe berries may be black or white depending on the variety.

Edible Parts

The berry is the edible part of the mulberry plant, and is famous for its sweet taste. Add mulberries to pies, baked goods, or eat raw by the handful! Adding mulberries to jams and preserves is another great way to keep enjoying their sweet flavour.

Notes

Do not eat unripe mulberries, as they are very bitter and can cause severe stomach aches in large quantities.

Russian Olive (Elaeagnus Angustifolia)

Russian olive is an invasive species in the Pacific Northwest and grows abundantly: You won't have any trouble finding it!

Identifying Characteristics

Russian olive trees have greyish-brown bark, with dark brown or red brown flexible branches. They can grow to a height of approximately 20 feet. The branches sometimes have spines. Leaves are long and pointed at the ends, and dull greyish-green in color. Before fruiting, the trees bear light yellow bell-shaped flowers. Fruits are oblong and grow at the ends of the branches. They are bright green when underripe, and are vivid orange-red with silver scales when ready to eat.

Edible Parts

Fruit can be eaten when completely ripe, raw or cooked. They are known for having a dry, mealy taste and texture, and are better as jams or pickles. The seeds inside the fruit can be roasted with seasonings.

Fig 14. Unripe salmonberries. From: Pixabay, by Lakeblog, 2021. https://pixabay.com/photos/salmonberries-unripe-6473360/. Copyright by Lakeblog/Pixabay, 2021.

Salmonberry (Rubus Spectabilis)

Identifying Characteristics

Look for salmonberries in moist, rainy forests, usually at or around the coast, riversides, or wetlands. The plant is most common in shadier areas, and takes the form of a leafy shrub between one and four metres long. Yellow, petalless flowers, which grow alone and not in clusters, may be present in some cases. The tops of new shoots are prickly as a defense mechanism. New shoots are green, but become red-brown and woody as they mature into the winter. The ripe salmonberry has a lively orange-red color and a compound appearance similar to a raspberry.

Edible Parts

Naturally, the tastiest part of the salmonberry plant is the ripe berries, which can be eaten raw or can make a great addition to jams, jellies, and preserves. Salmonberries are very soft and unsuitable for drying as they will lose their structural integrity and crumble. Unlike most other berry plants, the green shoots of a young salmonberry plant are edible when peeled, and can be eaten raw or cooked with grease or oil.

Sea Milkwort (Glaux Maritima)

Also referred to as sea milkweed, this lovely flowering plant conceals an edible rhizome at its root. Along with being a tasty addition to a fall meal, the sea milkwort rhizome has been used medicinally as a treatment for insomnia.

Identifying Characteristics

Look for sea milkwort growing along the coast, in places intermittently covered by the tide, in marshes, flooded meadows, and near other bodies of water. Sea milkwort grows in clusters or colonies, which vary in height from approximately 1 to 12 inches tall. The bright green stalks are thick and 'fleshy,' with stiff, oblong leaves covering the entire length. Pink or blush colored flowers are interspersed throughout the leaves and stalks. Each flower has four pointed petals arranged around a dark pink centre.

Edible Parts

The rhizome of sea milkwort, found at the root, is the only edible part of the plant, but should not be consumed raw. Boil in water until softened before eating (this may take a long time). Sea milkwort is traditionally consumed with butter or grease as a condiment.

Notes

Sea milkwort is known to make you sleepy and has been traditionally used for this purpose. Don't operate heavy machinery after consuming. Eating too much sea milkwort can lead to persistent drowsiness, nausea, or vomiting.

Self Heal (Prunella Vulgaris)

Considered a weed, this useful plant grows wild in many places around the world, including in the Pacific Northwest.

Identifying Characteristics

Look for self heal growing in damp soil, such as near rivers. The plant creeps along the ground instead of growing straight upwards. Stems are light green and branch near the top, where they bear dark green oval leaves in pairs on opposite sides of the stem. The calyx on top of the stem can be green or red and bears small hairs. Flowers are bright pink or fuschia and grow in a tubular shape.

Edible Parts

All parts of the self heal plant that grow above the ground are edible and also useful medicinally.

Fig 15. Stinging nettle leaves with distinctive serrated edges. From: Unsplash, by Paul Morley, 2018. https://unsplash.com/photos/JMuJfLVWtN4. Copyright by Paul Morley/Unsplash 2018.

Stinging Nettles (Urtica Dioica)

Anyone who enjoys exploring the outdoors has likely had an unpleasant encounter with stinging nettles, famous for the stinging or burning sensation produced by the hairs that cover the stalks and leaves. Surprisingly, parts of this prickly plant are very edible, and contain a high amount of calcium and iron.

Identifying Characteristics

Stinging nettle plants have one stalk, which is never branched and grows at an angle. Depending on the subspecies, the stem will be green or purple. The plant grows between 1.5 and 9 feet tall. Nettles tend to grow in rhizomatous colonies, though more uncommonly, you will see one plant alone. Look also for green or greenish-yellow clusters, especially at the tops. Stinging nettles have oval-shaped leaves, organized perpendicular to the shoots, with serrated edges.

The most identifiable part of the stinging nettle plant is the small hairs that produce the characteristic stinging sensation. These hairs can be seen (and felt) all over the leaves and shoots of most stinging nettle plants, though uncommonly, the shoots may not have hairs.

Edible Parts

To avoid irritating the skin of your mouth, choose younger, smaller stinging nettle plants to harvest. These have less irritant, and will also be less thick and bitter, making them tastier and easier to chew. Harvest young stinging nettles in the spring or fall for best results.

Both the leaves and shoots of stinging nettles are edible cooked, while young leaves are also edible raw. Cooked stinging nettles will not sting as the irritant does not survive the heat.

Notes

While the young leaves of stinging nettles are edible raw, if you eat them this way, their stinging hairs will still be active and may produce a mild stinging sensation as you eat.

The skin irritant produced by stinging nettles can get quite painful depending on how much you come in contact with. Always wear thick gloves to interact with stinging nettles and use a knife or shears when harvesting shoots.

Fig 16. A bull thistle plant in bloom. From: Unsplash, by Matt Seymour, 2020.
https://unsplash.com/photos/Awaf_6vEdtI Copyright: Matt Seymour/Unsplash 2020.

Thistle (Cirsium spp.)

There are a number of varieties of thistle located up and down the Pacific Northwest. Many farmers view this plant as a pest, as it can be dangerous to livestock. However, humans can eat many parts of the thistle plant, and it is among the easiest to find of the edible plants in the region.

Identifying Characteristics

The different varieties of thistle vary enough that it's worth addressing each of them separately. Overall, thistles grow in clusters of long, green stalks, topped with pinkish or purplish spiky round flowers. As weeds, they can grow almost anywhere, and may form patches in one location. The thistles in one patch will not necessarily all bloom at one time.

Canadian Thistle

Also known as creeping thistle, the Canadian thistle grows up t0 four feet tall and can be spotted by its extensive root systems that spread out widely from the plant. The leaves are bright green, spear-shaped, narrow, and barbed on the edges. Despite their spiky appearance, the leaves are soft to the touch. Like other thistle species, the flower is round and purple, and resembles a white dandelion head when it goes to seed.

Bull Thistle

By contrast to the Canadian thistle, the bull thistle's leaves are much darker in color and may have a bluish appearance. It has the distinctive round purple flower head when it blooms once every two years. Bull thistles are covered in very sharp thorns.

Indian Thistle

Indian thistle grows up to 10 feet in height and prefers to grow in moist regions. Plants consist of a single branching stem. The stem is hairy or fuzzy to the touch. The leaves are deeply lobed, giving them a 'toothed' appearance, and grow from leaf-like petioles extending from the stem. Flowerheads are very spiky, and white or pink in color.

Hooker's Thistle

Grows in clusters of short, stout stalks, covered in wool or fuzz that is soft to the touch. Flowers are white or cream, growing in spiky clusters at the top of the plant. Leaves are deeply lobed and spiny along the edges. Hooker thistle is a perennial and will grow back over multiple seasons when trimmed.

Edible Parts

The aerial parts of thistle are edible (remove thorns before cooking and eating if present!). Young flowerheads can be eaten cooked as they are very tough when raw, while stems and leaves are edible raw or cooked. Roots are edible in fall, and can be dried and ground into flour due to their high starch content. Roots can also be roasted or boiled.

Fig 17. Watercress in bloom. From: Pixabay, by alsen, 2014. https://pixabay.com/photos/watercress-blossom-bloom-spring-333746/. Copyright by alsen/Pixabay 2014.

Watercress (Rorippa Nasturtium Aquaticum)

Watercress is one of the best-known edible plants in the Pacific Northwest, known for its visually appealing white flowers and it's peppery taste. Add to summer salads to take the flavor up a notch!

Identifying Characteristics

Watercress will always grow in areas with still water, such as swamps, ponds, and marshes. Look for green, branching stalks that grow straight up, topped with small white flowers. The flowers have four square-shaped petals each, yellow centres, and grow in clusters.

Edible Parts

The entire watercress plant is edible raw. You can also steam watercress plants to soften them.

Notes

Before harvesting and eating watercress from a local pond or marsh, look online to see if there is a history of dumping or pollution in that body of water. Contaminants from garbage or chemical pollutants can be present in watercress from these areas.

Wild Chamomile (Matricaria Discoidea)

Famous for its sleep-inducing properties, chamomile grows wild throughout the Pacific Northwest! A common regional name for the plant is "pineapple weed."

Identifying Characteristics

Wild chamomile grows in recently disturbed, rocky soil. If you're familiar with the smell of regular chamomile, wild chamomile has a very similar fragrant odor. Look for short, branching green stems topped with petaless greenish-yellow flowerheads. The plant should be no taller than four inches. The leaves have a spiky, feathery appearance and cover the branches of the stem.

Edible Parts

The entire wild chamomile plant is edible. The most common use is to make herbal tea out of the flowerheads, which has the calming properties of regular chamomile.

Notes

Wild chamomile is thought to have a sweeter taste and fragrance than regular chamomile.

Fig 18. Yarrow flowers. From: Unsplash, by Olli Kilpi, 2020. https://unsplash.com/photos/PRWPNWnS4eU. Copyright Olli Kilpi/Unsplash, 2020.

Yarrow (Achillea Millefolium)

Considered one of the most medicinal herbs in the word, this unassuming flower is found growing wild throughout the Pacific Northwest and beyond.

Identifying Characteristics

Yarrow grows in wet soil in a variety of regions. Blooming in the summer, the yarrow plant is 12-24 inches tall at maturity. The stems are green and topped with flat disks or clusters of flowers. Yarrow flowers can be white, pink, or yellow. Leaves are hairy and alternately placed along the stem, growing smaller in size towards the top.

Edible Parts

The parts of yarrow that grow above the ground are edible. It's often included in infusions or eaten raw, though it can also be used as a potherb.

Notes

See Chapter 7 for some of the amazing medicinal uses of this common plant. Yarrow has been used for a vast range of medicinal purposes, including treatment of colds and flu, stopping bleeding, and breaking fevers.

Mushrooms and Fungi

Apricot Jelly Mushrooms (Guepinia Helvelloides)

These aesthetically pleasing mushrooms are hard to miss on the forest floor because of their lively apricot color.

Identifying Characteristics

Look for apricot jelly mushrooms in shady forested regions after summer and fall rains. These mushrooms are almost always found near coniferous trees, especially where there is rotting conifer wood nearby. These lovely fungi always grow in groups. The mushrooms are small, around two to three inches in diameter, with a bright color that ranges from apricot to pink. The fruits of the mushrooms are gelatinous and rubbery to the touch, with a curved petal-like or trumpet shape.

Edible Parts

Always cook apricot jelly mushrooms before eating. The above-ground parts of the mushrooms can be eaten, and are said to have a sweet but subtle flavor.

Fig. 19. A mature cauliflower mushroom. From: Pixabay, by kfalk, 2016. https://pixabay.com/photos/mushroom-spongy-cauliflower-mushroom-1784177/ Copyright kfalk/Pixabay 2016

Cauliflower Mushrooms (Sparassis spp.)

The "cauliflower mushroom" refers to a group of mushroom varieties that all strongly resemble their vegetable namesake. While not the prettiest mushroom to look at, these large edible mushrooms are tasty enough to be on any forager's radar.

Identifying Characteristics

Cauliflower mushrooms, like oyster mushrooms and chicken of the woods, grow on the wood of living trees. Look for cauliflower mushrooms on the lower part of pine trunks, near the roots, as they feed both on living trees and dead root matter. The fruiting body of the cauliflower mushroom is white, light brown, or tan, and has a wrinkled, spongy appearance similar to cauliflower. The smallest mature cauliflower mushrooms are about the size of your fist, but some can get as big as a basketball or larger.

Edible Parts

The aerial parts of the cauliflower mushroom are all edible when cooked. Since they have so many ridges and wrinkles, use a vegetable brush to be sure you're removing all dirt and debris before cooking.

Notes

While you should never eat a plant or mushroom you have not positively identified, there are no poisonous look alikes to the cauliflower mushroom in the Pacific Northwest. Cauliflower mushrooms are perennial, so if you harvest them carefully with a mushroom knife, you should be able to come back to the same place and find more next season.

Fig 20. Chicken of the woods. From: Pixabay, by Perkons, 2017. https://pixabay.com/photos/sulphur-mushroom-2362179/. Copyright Perkons/Pixabay 2017.

Chicken of the Woods (*Laetiporus Sulphureus*)

These mushrooms, also known as sulphur mushrooms, are known for growing on the trunks of damaged trees. Unlike other mushrooms, they're known for their unique 'shelf' appearance, as well as their vivid colors.

Identifying Characteristics

Look for chicken of the woods growing on tree trunks that have been scratched, dented, or split. These mushrooms get quite large, ranging from 2 to 10 inches in diameter. Instead of having a distinct cap and stem, the mushrooms grow in layers of 'shelves.' If you look closely, you can see the shelves are made of tightly-packed small filaments. While younger shelves have a lively orange-yellow color and a soft, moist, squishy texture, older shelves are pale in color, chalky, and brittle.

Edible Parts

The younger and smaller shelves of the chicken of the woods mushrooms are edible by humans. These should be cooked before eating.

Chicken of the woods absorbs nutrients from the trees it grows on. Some of these compounds can cause an allergic reaction in some people. Older chicken of the woods specimens have higher amounts of this compound, so choose smaller, younger shelves when harvesting, and start by eating a small amount.

Fig 21. Common puffballs. From: Pixabay, by kleijweg1, 2019. https://pixabay.com/photos/fungi-forrest-nature-decorative-4501878/. Copyright by kliejweg1/Pixabay 2019.

Common Puffball (Lycoperdon Perlatum)

Common puffballs are an easy-to-find mushroom species with an adorable round and fluffy appearance.

Identifying Characteristics

The common puffball is odorless and white or off-white in color, with no spots or patches anywhere on its body. It has no ridges or gills, and a firm texture when poked. The cap is round, directly attached and does not hang over the stem. The common puffball gets its name from the small spines that cover the surface of the cap, which are conical in shape. These spines may have black tips. Rubbing off the spines leaves behind a pattern resembling a grid or net.

Edible Parts

The common puffball's stems and caps can both be eaten when cooked.

Notes

The presence of the spines is essential to distinguishing the common puffball from other non-edible species. Reject a specimen if it does not have spines, if it is patchy or varies in color, or if it has an unpleasant odor.

Fairy Ring Mushrooms (Marasmius Oreades)

In the past, mushrooms growing in rings were thought to indicate places where fairies danced at night. Stepping inside of a ring was said to put a person at risk of being kidnapped by the fairies. While most of these beliefs have died out in modern times, their influence can still be seen in the name of these common edible mushrooms that are known for growing in rings.

Identifying Characteristics

Fairy ring mushrooms are found in meadows and fields, and grow in rings or semicircles. The mushrooms are tan to light brown on the outside with white flesh on the inside and slender stems. Caps are roughly 2 and a half inches in diameter and convex-shaped. Older mushrooms, which are less edible, have caps that resemble UFOs or an upside-down saucer with a darker hump on top. The undersides of the caps have distinctly veiny gills. Fairy ring mushrooms can be distinguished from certain inedible lookalikes by confirming that the stem is solid, not hollow.

Edible Parts

Fairy ring mushroom stems and caps can be eaten cooked, but are unsafe to eat raw. Do not eat fairy ring mushrooms found near a roadway: They may be contaminated.

Horn of Plenty (Craterellus Cornucopioides)

Also known as the black chanterelle or black trumpet, these mushrooms are highly valued by cooks for their beautiful dark appearance and rich flavor.

Identifying Characteristics

These mushrooms will always be found growing in groups or patches. Similarly to other types of chanterelle mushrooms, horns of plenty are distinguished by their heads, which look like a trumpet or funnel. These turn outwards at the tops, revealing the appearance of the inside. The outsides of the mushrooms are ashy or bluish grey in color, not ridged or gilled, and slightly wrinkled. The insides of the funnels have a rough or scaly texture and vary in color between brown, grey, and black.

Edible Parts

The horn of plenty trumpet and stem are edible when cooked. These mushrooms are commonly paired with chicken and used in gourmet dishes. Try them in a polenta or pasta sauce to make the most of their flavor!

Notes

Older horn of plenty trumpets develop cracks and waves down the sides. It is never recommended to eat an overripe mushroom, so choose specimens with their trumpets intact instead.

Fig. 22 King bolete mushroom. From: Pexels, by Roman Pohorecki, 2021. https://www.pexels.com/photo/brown-mushroom-16706/ Copyright Roman Pohorecki/Pexels 2021.

King Bolete (Boletus Edulis)

The king bolete mushroom is a large mushroom variety known for some unusual characteristics, such as not bruising when cut.

Identifying Characteristics

King bolete mushrooms are found in forested regions during the fall months when the ground is covered in leaves. Look for mushrooms with wood brown to reddish brown caps that are flat on top. The undersides of the caps are distinctive in that they are covered in pores rather than ridges or gills. The pores should be soft and squishy to the touch. Stems are ivory, off-white or cream in color, thick, and have a white 'network' growing on the outside. While most mushroom species bruise a bluish color when cut or crushed, king bolete mushrooms do not, and can be distinguished from some inedible varieties this way.

Edible Parts

The above-ground parts of king bolete mushrooms are edible when cooked.

Notes

While there are no bolete varieties that will kill you, poisonous look-alikes to the edible king bolete can cause vomiting and stomach pain if consumed. Ensure that your king bolete mushrooms do not bruise when cut and that there is no red or pink tinge on the underside of the caps.

Fig 23. Morel mushroom. From: Unsplash, by Beth Macdonald, 2020.

https://unsplash.com/photos/xHwRfau81rE. Copyright by Beth Macdonald/Unsplash 2020.

Morel (Morella spp.)

These delicious mushrooms have an unusual hollow interior and distinctly nutty taste.

Identifying Characteristics

To identify a morel mushroom, look for an oval-shaped brown cap covered in inward pits. The shape of the cap and the size of the pits should be uniform all over. The caps are entirely attached to the stem at the base and do not hang over it like most mushroom species. The stem is white or off-white and sturdy. You can identify morels by cutting open a specimen: Both morel caps and stems are entirely hollow inside.

Edible Parts

Both the cap and stem of the morel mushroom are edible. Morels are traditionally cooked in butter, which enhances the flavor.

Notes

The morel mushroom does have some inedible lookalikes. The best way to distinguish them is that morels will always be completely hollow inside both the cap and stem. While there are variants of morel where the cap is not completely attached to the base, do not eat these as they are too difficult to distinguish from other species.

Fig 24. Oyster mushrooms growing on a tree. From: Pixabay, by NatureFriend, 2013. https://pixabay.com/photos/mushrooms-mushroom-tree-trunk-295823/ Copyright NatureFriend/Pixabay 2013.

Oyster Mushroom (Pleurotus Ostreatus)

Oyster mushrooms are cultivated all over the world, but are just as delicious when harvested from the wild. These mushrooms grow directly on the side of hardwood trees and are highly valued for their savoury flavor in a number of Asian cuisines.

Identifying Characteristics

The name of the oyster mushroom comes from its distinctive oyster-shaped cap. To distinguish oyster mushrooms from lookalikes, look at the trunks of hardwood trees such as oaks, maples, poplars, alders, and ashes for clusters of wide-capped mushrooms growing directly from the bark. Most oyster mushroom caps are broader than 3.5 inches. The undersides of the caps are covered in off-white gills, which descend down the stem to the base of the mushroom. The tops of the caps are beige, grey, or light brown, smooth, and have a soft appearance. The spore deposits range from lilac to shades of grey.

Edible Parts

The oyster mushroom cap and stem are both edible. Since they are a large mushroom species, they're best when cut up and sauteed or used in making sauces.

Notes

Only harvesting large mushrooms from the sides of trees helps you ensure that you are actually harvesting oyster mushrooms, and not a toxic look-alike. As well, be sure of the species of tree you are harvesting from before positively identifying a mushroom as an oyster mushroom as there are inedible lookalikes that grow on aspens, conifers, and cottonwoods. Do not harvest mushrooms covered in fuzz, with ruffled gills, or with gilless stems attaching them to the tree.

Fig 25. Closeup of a golden chanterelle. From: Unsplash, by Timothy Dykes, 2021.
https://unsplash.com/photos/pwE2OExLYc0 Copyright by Timothy Dykes/Unsplash 2021.

Pacific Golden Chanterelle

One of the beautiful varieties of chanterelle growing up and down the Pacific Northwest, the Pacific Golden Chanterelle makes a hearty addition to any fall dinner.

Identifying Characteristics

The Pacific Golden Chanterelle has a curved, trumpet-like appearance. The stem is thick, grows wider at the top, with the end resembling a trumpet mouth or the opening of a funnel. The trumpet has a rich golden color while the stem may range from pale yellow to gold as well. The underside of the trumpet is noticeably ridged, with the ridges forming forks and branches as they extend towards the outer edge of the mushroom.

Edible Parts

The entire Pacific Northwest Chanterelle is edible. Chanterelles are traditionally sauteed with butter or simmered in cream before being included in a pasta sauce or topping.

Notes

Be aware that there are look-alikes to the Pacific Golden Chanterelle that are poisonous when eaten. These mushrooms usually have gills, not forked ridges, on the undersides, as well as black, brown, or white spore deposits.

Chapter 2:

Poisonous Plants of the Pacific Northwest

While it is not recommended to try and use tests to determine if a plant is edible (instead, become familiar with varieties of edible and non-edible plants, and ensure that a plant has ALL of the traits of the species you think it is before harvesting), there are some situations where the best course of action in all cases is to discard the plant.

Mushrooms become inedible while overripe. Overripe mushrooms may have visibly rotting portions, cracked, torn, wavy, or crumpled caps or trumpets, visible discoloration or spots, or drooping appearances. Reject these specimens and choose younger ones instead.

Fig 26. Poison oak leaves. From: Unsplash, by James Whitney, 2019.
https://unsplash.com/photos/Z_JF_BjNbZY. Copyright James Whitney/Unsplash 2019.

Fig 27. Poison ivy leaves. From: Pixabay, by James DeMers, 2013. https://pixabay.com/photos/poison-ivy-toxicodendron-radicans-195123/ Copyright James DeMers/Pixabay 2013.

Poison ivy and poison oak grow throughout the Pacific Northwest. While generally non-lethal, these plants can leave you with an itchy rash if you touch them on the leaves or bark. An old saying on avoiding these plants is "leaves of three, leave it be." This refers to how the leaves of these plants are compounded and grow in three distinct sections that are easily mistaken for groups of three leaves. If you see a woody shrub or creeping vine where leaves are apparently growing in groups of three, avoid touching it, even in passing.

As mentioned above, never eat a plant or mushroom if you're even the slightest bit uncertain what it is, or if it's appearance varies from the list of traits provided. It is highly recommended to seek in-person instruction on identifying plants to accompany this guide. However, we've included descriptions of some common poisonous plants that are endemic to the Pacific Northwest to help you distinguish them from edible varieties. These are *not* all the poisonous plants that grow in this environment, but a selection of common varieties that share traits with edible species.

Plants and Herbs

Fig. 28 Holly leaves and flowers. From: Unsplash, by Alastair MacRobert, 2020.
https://unsplash.com/photos/vjdu7KWzKM0 Copyright Alastair MacRobert/Unsplash 2020.

American Holly (Ilex Opaca)

Don't mistake holly's red berries for edible varieties, as these plants are very poisonous. Holly is often added to decorations around Christmastime due to religious symbolism attached to the plant. While holly is perfectly safe to touch, eating it's attractive red berries can make you very sick.

American holly is an evergreen tree with branches arranged alternately along its trunk. The leaves are dark green and glossy on top, tough to the touch, oval-shaped, with spikes arranged around the edges. The undersides of the leaves are not glossy and have a paler green color. The tree has a pyramid shape with longer branches on bottom progressing to smaller ones on top, and can reach heights of up to 60 feet. The holly tree bears small white flowers in spring and clusters of bright red berries through fall and winter. Flowers have four petals and yellow centres, while berries are very round and glossy in appearance.

Fig 29. Red baneberries. From: Pixabay, by Mike Goad, 2019. https://pixabay.com/photos/red-baneberries-bane-berries-3963764/. Copyright Mike Goad/Pixabay 2019.

Baneberry (Actaea spp.)

Both the red (Actaea rubra) and white (Actaea pachypoda) plants are highly toxic and common throughout North America, including the Pacific Northwest. Eating the berries from these bushes produces a burning sensation in the mouth, followed by dizziness, cramping, vomiting, and eventually respiratory and cardiac arrest.

Identifying Characteristics

Mature baneberry bushes reach a height of 36-48 inches and are covered in large saw-toothed leaves. The leaves have a feathery appearance and can be identified by a layer of fuzz on the undersides. Both species of baneberry bushes have long, broad-spanning roots and bear white flowers between May and June. Berries are ripe in late summer. The red baneberry species has thicker stems than its white counterparts and bear clusters of shiny red or white berries. White baneberries, by contrast, are always white with a distinctive black spot, which gives them the appearance of eyes.

Bittersweet Nightshade (Solanum Dulcamara)

Nightshade is commonly known as a poisonous plant, but do you know how to spot it in the wild?

Identifying Characteristics

Bittersweet nightshade flowers in late spring and early summer. The stems of bittersweet nightshade grow along the ground or climb vertically along another plant or rock and have a twisting, flexible, woody appearance. Mature plants are between three and nine feet long. Leaves are placed alternately along the stems and may have lobes extending to each side, giving the appearance of three leaves instead of one. In some variants, leaves are fuzzy on the undersides. Flowers are violet in color, with five petals forming a tubular shape and bright yellow conical pistons extending from the middle. The plant bears fruit in the late summer in the form of shiny red berries.

Fig. 30 Buttercup blossoms. From: Unsplash, by Ray Harrington, 2021.
https://unsplash.com/photos/MBeBLtuHOF0 Copyright Ray Harrington/Unsplash 2021.

Buttercups (Ranunculus spp.)

Buttercups are the subject of a common childhood game: If holding a buttercup under your chin reflects a yellow glow on your skin, it's said that you like butter! However, while they look unassuming, these attractive little flowers are not edible, and rubbing their leaves on your skin can cause irritation and blistering. Eating buttercup flowers or leaves can lead to dizziness, nausea, stomach pain, and even full or partial paralysis.

Identifying Characteristics

Buttercups can be found anywhere you would expect weedy plants to grow, such as in meadows and around disturbed soils. They come in a number of varieties, but most commonly, flowers are small, yellow, and bear five petals. Flowers are borne individually or in small clusters. Occasionally, buttercups will bear white flowers. Leaves are small, veiny, and alternately placed along the thin stems of the plant.

Fig. 31 A blooming hemlock plant. From: Pixabay, by JACKLOU-DL, 2020. https://pixabay.com/photos/plant-bush-stems-petals-hemlock-5502057/ Copyright JACKLOU-DL/Pixabay 2020.

Poison Hemlock (Conium Maculatum)

While the untrained eye may mistake poison hemlock for yarrow or a similar edible herb, this can be a costly mistake. These are extremely poisonous plants that can cause paralysis of the nervous and respiratory systems. You want to avoid even touching poison hemlock as the toxin can be absorbed through your skin. Poison hemlock toxin remains in dead plants for up to three years.

The stems of the poison hemlock plant are branched, characteristically hollow, thick, green, and streaked with red and purple. Stems are always smooth and free of hairs. Leaves grow from branches along the stems. Similarly to those of ferns, leaves are bright green, divided, and serrated along the edges. The small white flowers grow in clusters on the branched stems, with each cluster forming an umbrella or disk shape. Flowers have five petals each.

As poison hemlock is biennial, first and second year plants differ in appearance. First year plants are very short, lack flowers, and have additional red and purple blotches on the stems. Second-year plants are up to 6 to 10 feet in height and bear flowers.

Fig. 32 Snowberry clusters. From: Unsplash, by Annie Spratt, 2021.
https://unsplash.com/photos/FUmGvzRgrmM
Copyright Annie Spratt/Unsplash 2021.

Snowberry (Symphoricarpos spp.)

While these berries are beautiful to look at, be sure not to confuse them for mulberries or huckleberries as they are mildly toxic. While snowberries have been consumed by people in some cases and are a source of food for many grazing animals, eating them can make you sick because of their high quantities of indigestible saponins.

Identifying Characteristics

As a very hardy plant, snowberry shrubs can thrive on rocky outcrops and rough terrain. Snowberry shrubs can reach heights of three to nine feet tall, though some varieties spread out across the ground instead. The leaves are ovate in shape, bright green, and alternately placed along the branches of the plant. Before bearing fruit, the plant flowers in pink bell-shaped blossoms in the early spring. The berries are the most distinctive part of the plants, growing in bright white clusters at the ends of the branches.

Mushrooms and Fungi

Conocybe (Conocybe Tenera)

Looking extremely similar to the hallucinogenic Psilocybe mushrooms, these lethal mushrooms are very common throughout the Pacific Northwest.

Identifying Characteristics

Look for mushrooms with very thin, curved stems and conical caps. Caps may become slightly bell-shaped in older specimens. Caps range in color from ochre to darker rust-brown, and are smooth to the touch. In dry summer weather, caps may fade to pale yellow or beige. Stems do not have a ring around the middle. The undersides of the caps have a reddish-brown or rust-colored appearance and are covered in gills.

Deadly Galerina (Galerina Marginata)

Don't be fooled by the beauty of these smooth orange mushrooms; they're deadly poisonous when eaten. Deadly galerina mushrooms are so similar to some edible varieties in appearance that even edible mycologists can struggle to tell the difference. To keep yourself safe, it's best to avoid mushrooms with this appearance altogether.

Deadly galerinas can be found growing in small clusters on fallen wood, wood chips, mulch, or anywhere dead wood is decomposing. Occasionally, they will grow as individuals. These mushrooms are highly praised for their striking beauty. Their caps are yellowish or orangish brown in color and very smooth to the touch, without wrinkling or fraying (though damage can be seen in older specimens). The shape of the caps ranges from slightly convex to almost flat. Stems are brown and covered in white fibrils. The color of the stem darkens as the mushroom ages. When crushed, deadly galerinas produce a foul, musty-smelling powder.

Fig 33. A mature death cap mushroom. From: Pixabay, by vjgalaxy, 2019. https://pixabay.com/photos/mushroom-poisonous-amanita-4643456/. Copyright 2019 by vjgalaxy/Pixabay.

Death Caps (Amanita Phalloides)

There is no antidote to death cap toxin, which sets in within 24 hours of consumption. Immature death caps, covered in a membranous veil, resemble common puffballs.

Identifying Characteristics

Death caps grow near leafy trees, such as oaks, and prefer to grow in shade. Adult death caps are greenish, yellowish, or white in appearance, with broad, flat caps that have gills on the undersides. Young death caps have white bulb, dome, or egg-shaped caps, which are attached to the stem with a 'veil.' This veil breaks off as the cap expands and flattens, giving the appearance of a wavy skirt or ring around the middle of the stem. Gills are visible on the underside of mature death cap caps. Death caps have a distinctive bulbous vulva, or cup-like structure, at the base of the stem.

Destroying Angel (Amanita Bisporigera, Amanita Ocreata)

Destroying angel mushrooms are very similar in appearance to death caps, but an inexperienced eye may also mistake them for the edible common puffball. Stay safe while foraging by learning to spot the difference.

Identifying Characteristics

Similarly to the edible common puffball, destroying angels are white or off-white. Caps may have a tanned, pinkish, or yellow center and a curved bump on top. Mature destroying angel caps can be up to four inches across. Destroying angels may be mistaken for common puffballs because for much of their development, the entire mushroom is covered by a membranous vulva that breaks as they mature. Like death caps, this gives them a wavy ring attached to the middle of the stem. The stem retains the bulbous vulva after the membrane breaks. In mature mushrooms, the underside of the caps have gills that are not attached to the stem.

Notes

Immature destroying angels and death caps both strongly resemble common puffballs. The main distinction is the presence of the bulbous vulva at the base of the stem in these toxic species, which can be viewed by picking a mushroom and slicing open the sac.

Fig: 34 False morels with brain-like heads. From: Pixabay, by artellliii72, 2021. https://pixabay.com/photos/morels-mushrooms-spring-nature-6241791/ Copyright artellliii72/Pixabay 2021.

False Morels (Gyromitra spp.)

"False morels" refers to a group of mushroom variants that are easily mistaken for the sought-after morel mushroom. While these toxic varieties can look very similar to the morel, they are easily distinguished by paying attention to a few key features. False morel poisoning can lead to nausea, vomiting, dizziness, fainting, headaches, and eventual death, so it's important to be able to tell these mushrooms apart!

Identifying Characteristics

False morels are commonly said to be very ugly in comparison to their edible cousins. The caps are reddish brown or dark brown, and covered in wrinkles and folds. Many people say that false morel caps resemble human brains. While edible morel caps are covered in deep pits divided by ridges, false morel caps lack these and are brittle to the touch. Like morels, false morel stems are cream or off-white in color. Unlike morels, false morels are not completely hollow on the inside. Some inedible varieties may be completely solid, while others may have hollow chambers, but true edible morels are always completely hollow. Cutting open a specimen is the quickest way to distinguish inedible impostors from regular morels.

Notes

While some claim that there are ways that you can prepare false morels to eat them safely, false morel poisoning is serious enough that this should not be attempted under any circumstances.

If You've Accidentally Eaten a Poisonous Plant

If you accidentally consume a poisonous plant, it's important to take action right away to prevent serious illness, permanent damage, or death. If every precaution is taken and plants are not eaten unless they have been positively identified, this situation *should not occur*. However, in the event that you realize that you or someone else has eaten something inedible, the steps you should take are included here. This guide should be reviewed before you go foraging to ensure you know the steps to take in an actual emergency.

Step One: Stop Eating

While this should be obvious, if you are experiencing symptoms of poisoning or realize you have wrongly identified the plant, the first thing you should do is stop eating the plant and anything it's come in contact with. Don't try to make yourself vomit unless recommended by Poison Control or a medical professional: Poisonous plants can also be harmful on the way up. Ensure none of the plant is left in your mouth and rinse with water if you have time to do so. Immediately tell anyone you're with what's happening to alert them to the situation and ensure they do not also eat the plant.

Step Two: Call 911 or Poison Control

If you are experiencing symptoms of poisoning (a handy list of which is included below), call 911 immediately. Upon calling 911, the first thing you should tell the dispatcher is "I need an ambulance. I'm at (your address here)," before explaining the situation. Seconds can matter, and this way allows the dispatcher to send you help as quickly as possible. Tell the dispatcher that you may have been poisoned and request immediate medical assistance. Answer all questions to the best of your ability and follow their instructions.

However, if you realize you have misidentified a plant and are not feeling symptoms, especially if you've only eaten a small amount, you can call Poison Control at 1-800-222-1222. Explain the situation, including what you thought the plant was and where you got it. As before, the dispatcher may ask questions and/or provide instructions. Cooperate with them to the best of your ability.

Step Three: Bring the Plant With You

If you tell 911 or Poison Control that you've eaten a poisonous plant, they may send an ambulance or recommend that you make your way to the hospital. If this is the case, bring the plant with you in a container or Ziploc bag if at all possible. This will help medical professionals confirm what you ate and what the treatment should be. Taking pictures of plants before harvesting can also help in this situation.

Symptoms of Plant Poisoning

If you have one or more of these symptoms after eating a wild plant, it may have been poisonous. Follow the steps from the section above immediately to ensure you get treatment before it's too late.

- Feeling drunk, dizzy, or nauseous

- Blurry or distorted vision

- Stomach pain

- Difficulty walking or talking

- Vomiting or diarrhea

- Irregular heartbeat or a heartbeat that is too fast or slow

- Breathing trouble

- Swelling of the mouth and throat

- Rashes or hives

Chapter 3:

The Foragers Backpack

Not every forager's backpack will look the same. Foraging on your own property or in well-trafficked areas will not require you to pack as much as a daylong or multi-day hike in the wilderness. Use discretion and common sense when packing your bag, but when in doubt, remember that it's better to have and not need than need and not have! This chapter provides some insight into the tools that foragers may choose to invest in, and finishes with two examples of the equipment that two different foragers might bring on their expeditions.

The Backpack

Fig 35 Two large backpacks for hiking. From: Unsplash, by S.B Volanthen, 2017.
https://unsplash.com/photos/D75_5tWZDQ4 Copyright S.B Volanthen, 2017

Especially for those venturing deeper into the wilderness, your backpack is something you don't want to cheap out on. While backpacks are available at a range of prices, it's worth noting that investing in a good one will not only make your foraging expeditions easier as you'll be able to comfortably bring everything you need, but will also save money in the long run as you'll be able to use the same one for years before needing to replace it. It also helps you to make your other equipment last longer as you'll be able to take care of them. Good hiking backpacks have pockets and compartments that allow the safe packing of a number of things, so everything won't be bumping together in the main part of the bag.

Foragers who are hiking into the wilderness will want to select a high-quality backpack large enough to carry their essential equipment as well as their harvest. Multi-day hikes usually call for a 25 to 35 litre backpack in order to carry a tent and cooking supplies, but 10 to 20 litres is most suitable for a hours or day-long hike. If you pack your things in strategically, you should still have plenty of room for your harvest.

There are a couple of traits that good hiking backpacks have in common. Backpacks intended for multi-day hikes with a lot of gear should have a *suspension system*, which distributes the weight of a heavy pack comfortably across your back, but this isn't necessary for 10 to 20 litre packs in most cases. Look for wide, comfortably padded straps that don't dig into your shoulders. Many backpacks also have foam or mesh lining that goes against your back and on the undersides of the straps, which allows air ventilation that will prevent the uncomfortable buildup of sweat. A rain cover, which is a water resistant flap that can be used to cover the outside of the bag, is an absolute necessity in the Pacific Northwest!

On the inside, look for a valuables pocket (this should be small and zippered) for a place to put your phone, as well as inner and outer compartments for storage of different pieces of gear and containers. Your backpack should have enough compartments to store your entire kit in a manner that gives each thing a designated place, including a designated sleeve for your water bottle.

If you're staying in well-trafficked and populated areas, you might find a full-size backpack cumbersome and unnecessary, but in these cases you might want something smaller that's durable enough to carry the essentials. If you're not going into the wilderness (such as if you're foraging on your property, in green spaces throughout your town, or at the edges of roads), you can get away with a small water resistant pack instead of a full hiking pack. This would allow you to bring an extra sweater, water bottle, snacks, your tools, mini first-aid kit, and a couple of containers with ease. Same as with a full hiking backpack, look for one that is comfortable and doesn't chafe when you move.

Reaping the Harvest – Tools For Harvesting Wild Plants

Baskets and Containers

Baskets are well-loved by foragers, as they allow you to stow your harvest as you pick it without having to stop and fumble with a container with a lid. Furthermore, while this shouldn't be your first concern, many foragers love the classically appealing look of a basket brimming with a fresh harvest. Baskets are a great way to carry back a harvest from nearby your home, when you won't be hiking a long time over difficult terrain and might not have a full-size backpack on you. They are also usually made of natural materials, allowing you to cut back on your use of plastic, and they can be reused again and again. Buying a locally-made basket is a great way to support local artisans. On the flip side, there are several reasons why you might *not* choose to bring a basket foraging. Their bulky size makes it less feasible to take with you on a long hike. Most baskets can only be carried in your hands, making them a bit much to deal with if you're trying to navigate rocks and roots on the ground at the same time, though occasionally you will find varieties with a strap that allow you to put them across your back or shoulder. If the place where you're foraging has a smooth walking path, and is not too far from your home or car, a basket can be an excellent option. Choose a basket with a very tight weave, as this will ensure that your entire harvest stays inside.

Depending on the size of the plant parts you harvest, metal containers are also a durable option. These are usually hardier than plastic containers, and better for the environment as well. Furthermore, you can stack metal containers inside of each other when they're empty, meaning they'll take up less space in your bag, and they are relatively lightweight in comparison to glass varieties.

You can also find leather, canvas, or nylon pouches that are intended for foragers to use to store their harvests, especially mushrooms and smaller herbs. The upsides of these are that they are flat when empty, making them easy and non-cumbersome to carry. Some of them, such as canvas mushroom pouches, are conveniently made to clip onto your backpack or belt. The biggest downside is that thinner (such as nylon) varieties of these bags don't protect the plants inside from being crushed by everything else in your pack, so be sure to place them at the top or in an outside pocket of your bag if you go this route!

Knives and Shears

Knives are extremely helpful to every forager. They allow you to harvest plants or parts of plants while minimizing how much you directly touch the parts you aren't taking with you, reducing the chance that you'll harm yourself on thorns, stinging nettle toxins, or other plant defenses. Knives also reduce how much you have to rip or tear plants while harvesting, allowing you to collect parts of plants while minimizing the damage to the whole. For example, a knife allows you to collect the younger shoots of a plant without having to rip them up, disturbing the older shoots around them. A serrated knife can be used to cut through thicker shoots or small branches if necessary. These knives can come in folding or sheathed varieties, but either way, make sure that you have a way of stowing the blade of the knife so you don't cut yourself on it while rummaging in your pack.

A mushroom knife is useful for cutting off a mushroom stem and cap without disturbing the rest of the mushroom colony (more on this in the next chapter). These are generally small folding knives with curved blades that are perfect for mushroom stems.

Shears, which function much like scissors, make it easier to clip off leaves, flowerheads, buds, or other plant extremities without ruining the entire branch or shoot. Pick a compact pair of garden shears with a sheath to protect the blade (and your hands), or one of the many intended for foragers available online!

As implied above, take care of your knives and make sure they are sharp before you head out. A blunt or dull knife is very dangerous, as they are much more likely to slip and injure you. Knife sharpening services can be found in your area with a quick Google search, but if you're comfortable, you can also learn to do it yourself with online tutorials.

Gloves

A thick pair of gloves is an essential part of any safe forager's gear. Wearing gloves is your best defense against plant defenses, such as stinging nettle toxins, thorns, and unexpectedly sharp plant parts. Furthermore, wearing gloves can stop you from injuring yourself in the event that your knife or shears slip.

Gloves for foragers can be made of a number of different materials, both natural and synthetic. Goatskin gloves are highly valued by foragers for their flexibility and durability.

Especially in the cooler months, bringing along a pair of woolen gloves on a longer hike will ensure you can keep your hands warm in the event you get lost.

Staying Safe

Proper Clothing

Dressing for the weather and terrain is essential not only to having the best experience, but also to keeping yourself safe.

It's generally recommended that hikers dress in layers, and the same goes for foragers who are hiking into the wilderness to look for their harvest. Dressing in layers allows you to easily modify how warm your clothing is if the weather changes. For example, instead of a T-shirt and one heavy coat for hiking on a brisk autumn day, you might wear a long sleeved shirt, a zip-up sweater, and a warm vest on top. Long pants are preferable to shorts, even in the summer, as they protect your legs from insect bites and scratches from branches and brambles.

Your footwear is also extremely important to staying safe throughout your foraging trip. Even if you're staying close to home, choose sturdy, closed-toe shoes with ankle support. Sandals can easily allow injuries from sharp rocks and brambles, while shoes without adequate ankle support increase your risk of twists and sprains. If you're hiking into the wilderness, choose a strong pair of hiking boots with sole treads that will prevent you from slipping on a muddy path or while climbing hills. These should be water-resistant and fit snugly, without rubbing or chafing. Like your backpack, hiking boots are an area where investing money in a good pair can save you money and inconvenience in the long run.

As mentioned above, many parts of the Pacific Northwest are mountainous. If you're hiking through the mountains, be aware that the weather in these regions can change on a dime. While you should always be dressing in layers, bringing along an extra change of clothes (including socks) and a rain jacket or waterproof coat can help stave off hypothermia in the case you get wet and can't get back to civilization immediately.

If you're foraging in the wilderness, be aware that other people may be hunting there. For this reason, dress so that you are not mistaken for an animal by wearing bright colors. A visibility vest can also be worn, as this will not only distinguish you as a human, but also make you easier to see at night or in poor weather conditions in the event that you get lost.

Water Bottle and Snacks

Regardless of how far you're going, you should bring water along. While a regular plastic water bottle can be suitable if you're staying within or very close to populated areas, if you're going on a hike, you need something a little bigger and sturdier. Choosing a metal or plastic reusable water bottle makes sure that you have enough water for your trek in a reliable container that won't break. Both metal and plastic water bottles are generally dishwasher safe, and great models are available made out of both materials.

Plastic reusable water bottles are valued for how light they are: They won't be adding much weight to your backpack when they're empty. Furthermore, many plastic water bottles come with measuring lines on the side so you can see how much you're consuming. The most popular brand of plastic water bottle is the classic Nalgene, which is known for being practically indestructible. If the Nalgene is outside of your price range, there are plenty of cheaper alternatives available. Look at your local hiking store or online for one that suits your needs!

Some people prefer to drink out of a metal water bottle and find them easier to clean. Metal water bottles also come in insulated varieties that can keep your water cold if you prefer that. However, some metal water bottles are heavier than their plastic counterparts, so keep this in mind while choosing yours.

Bringing snacks along gives you peace of mind that in the event you get lost, you won't also be starving. Furthermore, if you're hiking more than a couple of hours into the wilderness, having a snack can give you a burst of energy to fully enjoy your trip into the woods. Snacks suitable for hiking should be high-calorie and high in fat and protein, as these nutrients give you energy and help you to feel full. Nuts and seeds, trail mix, protein and nut bars, beef jerky, and dried fruit are all popular hiking snacks that can easily be packed into your bag.

If you're going on a hike for a day or more in the wilderness, consider bringing along water purification tablets. These can be used to purify river water in the event that you're lost and you run out of water in the wilderness.

First Aid Kit

A first aid kit is essential for anyone who spends time in the wild. The mountainous and thickly forested Pacific Northwest can be treacherous territory for inexperienced hikers and foragers, and even the most experienced outdoors-people can sometimes find themselves in unexpected situations. Therefore, the safest course of action is to expect the unexpected and bring along what you need to treat minor injuries before you leave the woods.

Your first aid kit should be in a sturdy case and be clearly marked with a red cross. This allows it to be visible in poor conditions and indicates what it is in the event that you're too injured to communicate. Depending on how far into the woods you're going, the size of your first aid kit will vary. For example, someone foraging close to home should be okay with a very basic kit with one to two multiples of each size of bandage, while someone who hikes and camps deeper in the woods should pack more, in case of having to re-dress wounds multiple times over the course of a multi-day trek. Increase how much you carry again depending on the amount of people in your party.

Your first aid kit should include a set of sanitized tools, as well as supplies for dressing wounds. Standard first aid kits include:

- Tweezers

- Blunt-tipped scissors

- Small folding knife or scalpel

- Sterile gauze

- Adhesive bandages (band-aids) in assorted sizes

- Butterfly bandages in assorted sizes

- Splints and elastic wrap

- Climber's tape

- Antibiotic ointments

- Antiseptic wipes

Finally, look at the area you're foraging in and consider what other difficulties you might encounter. For example, a tick removal kit can be worth it to bring along if you're foraging in an area with grassy meadows and fields.

A survival blanket is a thin blanket made of a material that reflects back a high amount of heat, and can be folded into a tiny package when not in use. These are intended for emergency situations and are included in many first aid kits. If you're going into the wilderness, a survival blanket should definitely be on your "better safe than sorry" list, as they take up next to no room, but can save your life in a survival situation.

Map and Compass

Safe hikers should bring a compass with them on every trip, and this applies to foragers as well. While this might seem a little much, the thick forests and mountainous landscapes of the Pacific Northwest can be very easy to get lost in. If you're hiking in the wilderness, a compass can be used to keep track of what way you came from, helping you to find your way back if you get turned around and lose your bearings.

A map of the area is strongly recommended, even if you aren't going far. Looking for landmarks indicated on a map, in combination with a compass, is one of the best ways to keep track of where you're going, and to help yourself get back to where you need to be in the event you get off course. Furthermore, maps have non-emergency uses for foragers as well. Not only can a map show you where certain natural features are, helping you to find the plants you're looking for (for example, if you're looking for beargrass, you want to find an open and sunny hillside), but they can also indicate when you might be straying into a protected or private area.

Flashlight

Unless you plan on camping, it's generally unsafe to be out in the woods after dark. However, the first rule of wilderness safety is to be prepared for every eventuality, and even if you take all of the proper precautions to avoid them. Therefore, a flashlight is strongly recommended as part of your foraging kit, especially if you're hiking for a few hours or longer.

There are a number of different kinds of flashlights available on the market: some that are battery powered, powered by a hand crank, or even solar powered. If your flashlight is battery powered, bring a couple extra in your backpack just in case.

Even if you aren't out in the woods after dark, a flashlight can help you get a good look at mushrooms and other plants that grow in the dimmer areas at the base of tall trees! This allows you to forage more ethically by cutting down on the amount of plants that are needlessly damaged.

Phone and Power Bar

Most of us today spend our days attached to our phones, and heading out into the wilderness is a great way to unplug! However, even if you don't have it in your pocket, bringing your phone when you go foraging is important in keeping yourself safe. Not only does it allow you to call for help if you're lost and happen to still have service, your phone's flashlight can be used for signalling, and it also comes with a built-in compass.

Your phone should be in a sturdy case to allow it to survive falls when you're out in the woods. If you're really concerned about keeping your phone safe, there are waterproof phone cases and pouches on the market, which you can hang around your neck.

Before you head out, make sure your phone is fully charged and preferably in good repair. It's highly recommended to bring along a cord and a fully charged power bar as well. A power bar can give your phone another few hours of charge in the case that you get lost or injured, increasing the chances you'll be able to call for help.

Bear Spray

Bear spray is a must in grizzly country, and is also a good idea to carry along if you're going into the wilderness, in case of an encounter with another aggressive animal. More information on bear spray and how to use it can be found in Chapter 4.

Safety First: Rules to Remember

Time and Place

Time of Day and Weather Conditions

Before heading out to forage, check the forecast for the day. Clear or at least dry conditions are preferable for foraging. While a light rain shouldn't make things too difficult, be aware that wet conditions can make the ground muddy and slippery, leading to falls if you're traversing difficult terrain. Furthermore, mist and fog, especially in coastal wilderness regions, can obscure landmarks and make it harder for you to find your way back.

As you may have noticed in the first chapter, many edible plants in the Pacific Northwest grow along the coast and in mountainous regions. These are areas where the weather can change very quickly and unexpectedly. If you're out foraging in these locations and you notice that the weather seems to be taking a turn for the worse, the safest course of action is to pack it in if possible, regardless of what the forecast says.

Especially if you're heading into the wilderness, heading out earlier in the day is the best course of action as it increases the hours of daylight you have before dark in the event you're lost or injured. Foraging in the dark presents additional safety concerns such as trips and falls, not to mention potentially misidentifying plants in low-light conditions. Dangerous wildlife such as grizzly bears and cougars are also more active at dusk than they are during broad daylight.

Seasonal Changes

Along with the current weather conditions, the season when you forage can also make all the difference. Different plants are at their peak during different seasons, and what will be available differs depending on whether you head out during spring, summer, or fall. Furthermore, knowing when a plant is ripe can help to differentiate it from a look-alike. For example, it would be suspicious to see something that looked like a huckleberry bush bearing fruit in spring, when we know that these berries are ripe later in autumn! As we would not have space in this manual to go over when each and every plant in the Pacific Northwest is at its peak, some general rules to remember to help you find what you're looking for are included below.

Plants and herbs tend to be at their zenith between March and October, depending on the species. Stinging nettles, which can be eaten steamed or sauteed, are best when picked early in the spring. This is when the shoots of the plants are young and haven't had the chance to get harder and more bitter yet.

Most berries come into their peak in late summer and early fall. Most berry plants reproduce by enticing animals to eat their berries and spread the seed through their droppings. Therefore, this time of year is optimal for berry bushes to be ripe because many animals are fattening up for the winter. Raspberries, blackberries, and blueberries are at their zenith in the late summer (July and August), while huckleberries peak afterwards, between August and September. Salmonberries are one significant exception to this rule: These berries are ripest in May and June.

When it comes to foraging mushrooms, the optimal times are in the spring and the fall, depending on what species you're looking for. These are the times when the ground is the most moist, combined with the optimal temperature levels for mushrooms to grow. It's harder for mushroom colonies to precipitate during the brighter, drier summer season. Eating an overripe mushroom can be dangerous, so only forage for mushrooms that are in season.

A more detailed list of when to harvest the plants described in this book is provided below.

Foraging in the winter is much more difficult to do safely, even though some edible plants may still be blooming. The reason is that some plants, such as the red huckleberry bush, lose their leaves that can be used to distinguish them from inedible lookalikes. Snow and ice can also alter and obscure distinguishing traits of other edible plants. As being even 1% unsure about the identity of a plant means you should leave it alone, foraging in winter makes it much harder to come back with a safe harvest. Furthermore, winters in the Pacific Northwest are cold and wet, and going out in winter puts you much more at risk of encountering adverse conditions such as icy walking paths, black ice, and snow drifts.

List of Plants and When to Harvest

Agoseris: Flowers from July to August, goes to seed immediately afterwards.

Beargrass: Available year-round, but best in spring and summer.

Bedstraw: Late spring and early summer, only harvest when flowering.

Broadleaf Plantain: Flowers from June to September, goes to seed afterwards.

Cattails: May to July for the cigar-shaped head of the plant, later in summer for green flowerheads with seed capsules, late autumn for the roots.

Chickweed: Blooms in both mid-summer and fall, though the fall harvest is tougher and less palatable.

Devil's Club: Early spring, exact month varies depending on the area. The harvest window is very short..

Goldenrod: Late summer through September and sometimes October. Goldenrod is more bountiful when the weather starts to cool off.

Gooseberry: July to August in most cases, though can be harvested whenever the berries are ripe.

Horsetails: Early spring for the shoots, late spring for green tops. By fall, shoots will be ready to harvest again, but too tough to use for anything but tea.

Huckleberry: Best harvested in fall, August to September.

Indian Pipe: Flowers between late spring and fall.

Knotweed: May to November, exact time varies depending on the region.

Lady Fern Fiddleheads: Must be harvested while leaves are still curled, usually in March and April, but varies depending on the region.

Miner's Lettuce: Available in cool, rainy weather, from late winter through the spring. The harvesting window is longer depending on how damp and shady the site is.

Mulberry. July through September, though it varies based on the region.

Russian Olive: Blooms from May to June, after which flowers transform into fruits in the summer.

Salmonberry: Ripe in early spring, May to June.

Sea Milkwort: Flowers from June to August, but is a perennial, allowing you to potentially harvest more than once.

Self Heal: Best to harvest in the early summer before it blooms, but can be harvested whenever it's growing.

Stinging Nettles: Best to harvest in spring and early summer (May to June in some regions) before the plant blossoms.

Thistle: Late summer to early fall for aerial parts. Thistle flowers growing in a patch may also bloom at different times, allowing you to come back and harvest more than once. Roots can be harvested in fall.

Watercress: Harvest in spring for freshest and most tender leaves. Watercress will grow back over the summer, allowing a second harvest in the fall.

Wild Chamomile/Pineapple Weed: A very hardy plant that can grow throughout the year, but should be harvested whenever yellow flowerheads are in bloom.

Yarrow: Flowers all through summer.

	J	F	M	A	M	J	J	A	S	O	N	D
Agoseris							▓	▓				
Beargrass				▓	▓	▓	▓	▓				

Bedstraw					■	■	■					
Cattails					■	■	■		■	■	■	
Chickweed					■	■	■	■	■			
Devil's Club				■	■							
Goldenrod								■	■	■		
Gooseberry							■	■				
Horsetails				■	■	■				■		
Huckleberry								■	■			
Indian Pipe						■	■	■				
Knotweed					■	■	■	■	■		■	
Lady Fern Fiddleheads			■	■								
Miner's Lettuce	■	■	■	■	■	■						
Mulberry							■	■	■			

Russian Olive					■	■	■	■				
Salmonberry					■	■						
Sea Milkwort						■	■					
Stinging Nettles						■						
Thistle								■	■	■		
Watercress				■	■	■			■	■		
Wild Chamomile	■	■	■	■	■	■	■	■	■	■	■	■
Yarrow						■	■					

List of Mushrooms and When to Harvest:

Apricot Jelly Mushrooms: May to November, especially after rains.

Cauliflower Mushrooms: July to October.

Chicken of the Woods: August to October, especially if trees have been damaged by storms or animals during the summer.

Common Puffball: August to October.

Fairy Ring Mushrooms: April to November.

Horn of Plenty: August to October.

King Bolete: September to November.

Morel: May to June.

Oyster Mushroom: Depends heavily on the region. Oyster mushrooms grow best in cool, rainy weather.

Pacific Golden Chanterelle: August to October.

	J	F	M	A	M	J	J	A	S	O	N	D
Apricot Jelly					▓	▓	▓	▓	▓	▓	▓	
Cauliflower							▓	▓	▓	▓		

Species												
Chicken of the Woods								●	●	●		
Common Puffball								●	●	●		
Fairy Ring				●	●	●	●	●	●	●	●	
Horn of Plenty								●	●	●		
King Bolete									●	●	●	
Morel					●	●						
Oyster	●	●	●	●	●	●	●	●	●	●	●	●
Pacific Golden Chanterelle								●	●	●		

Location, Location, Location

Wilderness areas are the most popular to forage in, hence most of this guide refers to the equipment and safety precautions required to hike in the wilderness. Foraging in the wilderness can be incredibly rewarding as a way to get back in touch with nature, learn about the beautiful ecology of the Pacific Northwest, and get some exercise all at once. However, hiking in the wilderness presents the most safety concerns of all the possible locations you could go foraging, such as adverse weather and the possibility of getting lost. Wildlife also poses a concern. How to avoid getting lost in the wilderness, as well as how to handle unexpected encounters with wildlife, are discussed in more detail in the sections below. Popular locations for wilderness foraging in the Pacific Northwest are included in the Additional Resources chapter.

If your property is located in an area with a lot of wild plants, you can see if there's anything edible growing on your property. This goes doubly for people who live in rural areas and have large properties, such as homesteaders and farmers. There are a number of safety advantages to foraging on your own property: You probably know the area and the terrain very well, so the odds of getting lost are slim to none as long as you stay on the land you own! Furthermore, you most likely know if there's a history of pollution on your land that could contaminate your harvest.

Along roadsides once you get out of cities, or in green spaces within cities, you might be able to find some wild-growing edible plants. However, there are a couple of concerns to keep in mind when you do this. If you forage along roadsides, be sure to wear a high-visibility vest to indicate to traffic where you are, especially if you're foraging in the evening. Finally, foraging inside city limits makes it doubly important that you wash your harvest thoroughly, as the plants may have come in contact with car exhaust or dogs marking their territory. Plants are only safe to eat when they're found at least 50 metres back from the edge of the road. Otherwise, assume that they're contaminated.

Before Heading Out

Heading out into the wilderness alone is not recommended. Rather than heading out alone for your first wilderness foraging expedition, why not bring along your partner, a friend, or a family member to share in the experience with you? While you're out together, make sure they're familiar with foraging safety, such as the rule to never eat an unknown plant, and avoid getting separated.

Hiking and foraging in a popular hiking location (be sure that it's permitted on that trail!) makes it much more likely that there will be maps of your location available to print off and take with you, as well as trails to follow in order to stay on track. Not only that, but many popular hiking trails come with estimates of how long it takes to walk them, allowing you to more efficiently plan your trip. Don't bring a map on your phone: You could be left high and dry if your device dies!

Before heading out, it's not only important that *you* know where you're going, but that someone else, such as a trusted friend or family member, also knows where you're going and when to expect you back. In the event that something goes wrong, this person will be able to raise the alarm for you when they don't hear from you at the proper time.

The handy checklist provided below can help you make sure you're ready before heading out to forage. If you're staying close to home, you can forgo some of the points here that are specific to wilderness foraging, but if you're heading into the woods or mountains, make sure that you can check off every box below before stepping out the door!

Checklist

- I have a plan for my foraging expedition, including where I'm going and how long I expect it to take.

- I've checked the weather conditions for the area where I'm foraging, and there's no sign of adverse weather events today, such as heavy fog or rain.

- Someone else knows where I'm going and when I expect to be back. They have my phone number, and, if I'm driving, my license plate number.

- I have packed my bag with all the tools I need for foraging, as well as my safety equipment, such as my flashlight, compass, map, and first aid kit.

- My first aid kit is up to date and fully stocked for the amount of people who are in my party.

- My phone is fully charged.

- I'm dressed properly, including long pants and sturdy hiking boots or closed-toe shoes.

- I have a hard copy of a foraging guide in my pack, with accurate lists of traits I can use to identify plants.

- I have sufficient containers, baskets, or pouches to carry my harvest.

- I have a full water bottle and snacks in my backpack.

- I have gloves to protect myself from thorns and other plant defenses.

Wildlife to Watch Out For

Fig 36. A grizzly bear. From: Unsplash, by John Thomas, 2020. https://unsplash.com/photos/FdKDKLoSa0M Copyright John Thomas/Unsplash 2020.

Bears

When someone thinks of dangerous wildlife in the Pacific Northwest, grizzly bears are probably the first species to come to mind. These apex predators can pose a significant threat to humans during an unwanted encounter, but you can keep yourself out of harm's way by practicing basic bear safety every time you head out.

There are two kinds of bears found in the Pacific Northwest. Black bears are smaller, with shorter claws and straighter faces and ears. Their front paw prints can be distinguished by having one toe set lower than the other four, much like a thumb. Grizzly bears, also known as brown bears, are the larger and more aggressive variety. A grizzly bear paw print has all five toes in a line across the top of the palm. They have longer claws, dished or flat facial features, and a noticeable hump between their shoulder blades.

The official website of the Pacific Northwest National Scenic Trail provides a guide with pictures to help tell these two species apart, which is of utmost importance during an encounter. They recommend distinguishing bears primarily by the features listed above, rather than by their size or color. While there have been rare reports of attacks from black bears, grizzly bears pose a much more significant threat. Before foraging on a trail or in a wilderness region, a quick internet search can inform you of the risk of encountering grizzly bears in the area.

Take every precaution to avoid a close encounter with a bear, especially in grizzly country. When hiking or camping in the Pacific Northwest, always ensure that food is secured in airtight containers to prevent bears from smelling it. When camping, secure your food off the ground at least 100 yards away from your campsite to avoid drawing bears to you. Don't hike at dawn or dusk, as this is when bears are most active.

Bears like to forage in berry bushes as much as humans, so keep your eyes open while berry picking and don't use headphones. If it appears that someone has been digging small holes around bushes on the ground, this is a sign that bears have been there. If you spot a bear that is more than 100 yards away and it hasn't noticed you, you can safely and quietly leave the area. However, if the bear sees you, or if you are closer than 100 yards, follow these rules to the letter to exit the encounter safely.

If you see a route that you can use to calmly and quietly leave the situation, do so without panicking or running. Watch the bear for signs of agitation. An agitated bear will sway or duck its head, pin back it's ears, huff loudly, and/or click it's teeth together. If the bear seems agitated, stop moving, as you wish to show it that you're not a threat. A bear that is standing on two legs is usually trying to get a better look at you and may not realize that you're a human, rather than an animal like a wolf that could be dangerous to it.

Talk quietly when faced with a bear, avoiding direct eye contact. Being loud or staring it down could be interpreted as threats. Only attempt to frighten the bear by making yourself big or yelling if it persists in approaching you. If the bear attacks, deploy your bear spray. If you don't have bear spray, fall to the ground face down and use your hands and backpack to protect your head and abdomen: The bear might lose interest if it was attacking in self-defense and you show you're not a threat. If it persists in attacking and you have no other option, fight back.

When heading into grizzly country, carrying bear spray is strongly recommended. This is a highly concentrated pepper spray in an aerosol format that can be easily placed in your pocket or a hip holster. As it is non-lethal and easy to learn to use, it is a much safer self-defense tool against bears than a firearm. Bear spray has also been found to stop bear attacks in a vast majority of attempts, and is more effective in this than firearms. Following the instructions on the bottle, which should be reviewed beforehand, spray bear spray directly into the face of a charging grizzly bear. Leave the area at once while the bear is incapacitated.

Bear spray can also defend you successfully from attacks from other animals as well as bears, though it should only be used in an emergency.

Mountain Goats

Mountain goats are common in the hilly regions where many edible plants grow, so it's possible that you could come across one while foraging. Many mountain goats see people as a source of food, as like deer, uninformed people feed them. Furthermore, mountain goats love to lick salt, and if you're sweaty or carrying salty food, they may be drawn to the scent. For these reasons, it's possible that a mountain goat could approach you while you're in the wilderness.

If you need to urinate while foraging in the wilderness, do so at least 100 yards away from the trail or where you're harvesting plants so that goats aren't drawn to you by smelling the salt in your urine. Be aware that late October to December is mountain goat mating season, and males may act aggressively without any visible provocation during this time. Both sexes have sharp horns and can charge when threatened.

If you see mountain goats, the best course of action is to stay at least 50 yards away, and leave the area if possible to avoid looking like you're threatening them or want to feed them. If a goat approaches you, continue moving away. If a goat is acting aggressively or insists on following you, make yourself loud and scary by waving your arms, yelling, or throwing rocks. Always give the goat a route to leave the situation and avoid making it feel cornered.

Cougars

Also known as mountain lions or pumas, cougars are some of the most intimidating animals in the Pacific Northwest. Like mountain goats, most cougars are found in mountainous regions, as these areas allow them to optimize their hunting strategies by providing high places to pounce from. When you're foraging in these areas, talking out loud or to the people with you can alert any cougars nearby to your presence, giving it a chance to hide. Don't approach cougars if you see one. You don't want it to think you're threatening it or its den or kittens.

If you come face to face with a cougar by accident, don't panic. The cougar is more likely to attack if you turn and run. On the other hand, if you avoid showing fear, it would indicate to the cougar that you could put up a fight, making it less likely to attack you. Stand up straight, open your jacket, and spread out or wave your arms: This will make you look bigger and scarier. Join hands if you're with others, and pick up children. Speaking loudly and clearly in a firm voice, back away from the cougar slowly, showing it that you're not trying to corner it. If there's a way that the cougar could leave the situation, make sure you're not blocking its escape route. If the cougar starts to approach you, act louder and more aggressive to scare it off. If you're attacked, fight back: Try to strike the cougar on the head or nose as hard as you can. Use bear spray if you have it.

Chapter 5:

Protecting the Land: Guidelines for Ethical Foraging

In order to forage ethically, it's important to minimize damage to the environment. This includes the parts of a plant that you're not taking, as well as the plants around it. Furthermore, you want to avoid taking too much.

How to Harvest

Leaves, Buds, Shoots, and More

When harvesting extremities on plants, it's best to avoid damaging the branches or twigs you're collecting from, as plants are generally able to regrow these parts. The process of snipping off these parts is called pruning, and is something that is often done in gardens to help plants grow. If you prune wild plants carefully, they can continue growing as happily as before: Remember that these plants are almost all eaten by animals, and have evolved to survive the loss of a limited number of leaves and flowers. However, plants are better able to withstand pruning than others. As a general rule, the hardier and tougher a plant appears to be, the more pruning it can withstand. Furthermore, plants that are classed as 'weeds' regrow and spread very quickly and can grow almost anywhere, so you can prune off larger portions. When pruning off leaves, buds, and flowers, snip or cut at the base of the part you're removing, not the woodier part of the step or twig. This will allow the part to grow back.

The shoots of a plant refers to the stem-like structure that feeds water and nutrients from the soil into the upper leaves of a plant. Among plants with this structure, you can take a limited amount without killing the entire plant. Younger shoots are generally easier to harvest (and better tasting) as they have not had a chance to grow tough yet. When harvesting the shoots of a plant, use a folding knife or shears to cut off the younger shoots near the tops, while leaving the rest of the plant alone. Don't twist, rip, or tear at plant shoots, as you'll end up pulling out roots and damaging the plant as a whole.

A similar philosophy applies to picking perennial plants such as stinging nettles. Perennials will grow back if their roots are left intact. To harvest a perennial plant, simply snip or cut with your shears or knife to remove the plant without touching or damaging the roots. Don't pull it out!

Berries

Berries are the easiest part of a plant to harvest, as they do not require the use of any additional tools or much physical strength. You can pick berries by hand. Twist slightly as you pull off the part that you want in order to help detach it from the twig, stem, or branch without damaging it. Many berry bushes have thorns, so always use gloves to protect yourself while harvesting.

Berries that are overripe are less attractive to harvest, as they're likely to go bad before you have a chance to eat them all. Overripe berries will have a darker color, a soft or mushy texture, and a wrinkled or misshapen appearance. Underripe berries will be very hard, pink, white or green, and smaller than their ripe counterparts. Sometimes under-ripe berries can be useful in making jelly, but berries are safest to eat raw when fully ripe. In most cases, you want to choose berries at their peak ripeness for the best results.

Rhizomes and Whole Plants

The rhizome, which looks similar to a tuber or thick root, is the edible portion of some wild plants. These organs are responsible for initiating the growth of new roots, shoots, and stems. A section of the rhizome can be cut off of mature plants without killing the entire thing. To safely harvest rhizomes, dig at the base of your target plant until you can see the rhizome. Then, using a folding knife or shears, cut off a part of the rhizome (not the whole thing!)

and pull it out. Replace the dirt you dug away to protect the rhizome and roots you did not harvest.

If you're pulling out a whole plant (as you might want to in cases where the whole plant is edible, such as dandelions), check to see if it's entangled with any of the plants around it so that you don't pull out or damage them by mistake. Using gloves, grasp the plant firmly at the base and pull.

Mushrooms

While mushrooms look like a bunch of individuals growing closer together, in actuality, you are seeing parts of one organism. Mushrooms are connected underground as 'colonies,' therefore, when you see a group of mushrooms, you're actually looking at a single organism! The part of the colony that exists below the ground is called the mycelium, and is responsible for distributing water and nutrients to the above-ground "fruit bodies."

Therefore, when harvesting mushrooms, it's important to make sure you're not damaging the underground mycelium or you run the risk of killing the entire colony. The best way to do this is by using a mushroom knife, as these are perfectly curved to cleanly cut fruit bodies off where they meet the ground. If you don't have a mushroom knife, pinch and gently twist fruit bodies at the base to pick them.

Seeds

If you're interested in gardening, you may decide to retrieve seeds from wild plants to plant in your own garden. You may also want to harvest seeds from plants in order to eat them, such as in the case of broadleaf plantain. Seeds are ready to be harvested from wild herbs and flowers two to five weeks after they bloom. If you particularly liked a plant that you harvested ripe, try going back to it a few weeks later to see if it's bearing mature seeds. To harvest seeds from flowering plants and herbs, look for plants that are nearing the end of their lifestyle and have a drooping, wrinkled appearance. These may be forming seed pods, which look similar to pea pods, are usually grey or brown when mature and feel hard to the touch. Seeds can often be felt inside the pods. A mature seed pod should be able to easily snap off from the plant without twisting or tearing.

Some plants do not form seed pods, but have visible large seeds as they wilt at the end of their lifestyle. Seeds that are ready to plant will be brown, grey, or black in color with a hard shell on the outside. These are usually found in wilting flower heads or at the tops of stems. You should be able to gently shake or pick the seeds off of the flower or herb without having to tear or bend the plant.

With grassy or weedy plants, try using a fine-toothed metal hair comb to gently brush seeds from the stems of a plant at the end of its life cycle into a Ziploc bag or container. Like with herbs and flowers, if the seeds do not detach easily, it's too early to harvest them.

Fruit and berry seeds can be retrieved by separating them from the fruit itself. In the case of berries, these seeds can be very small, and you might have to crush down the fruit in order to pick them out. Some berry seeds are very small and you may have to use tweezers to manipulate them. Returning to a berry bush when the berries are well past their prime can make it easier to harvest seeds from wilting berries.

Some plants have seed pods at the tops of their stems that burst open at the end of their life cycle. If you notice round seed pods at the tops of plants like sea milkwort, one way to harvest these is to place a small mesh bag at the top of the plant when the seed pod is about to burst. Check back every other day to see if the pod has burst and the bag is filled with seeds. Always remember where a plant is when you do this, and never abandon the bag: Littering does real damage to environments!

Never plant seeds in a location where the plant is not a part of the native flora. The plant could spread and become invasive to the area, crowding out native plants and disrupting the ecosystem.

How Much to Harvest?

Most plants tend to grow in colonies, stands, or patches of the same species. Different foraging guides disagree on how much of a stand you should harvest, with recommendations ranging from ⅓ to 1/10. In most cases, ⅕ is an acceptable ratio. Follow this rule while taking parts of plants as well, such as a section of a rhizome or young shoots.

While the ⅕ ratio provides a solid rule of thumb when determining how much to take from a particular group of plants, there is a little more nuance to making sure that you don't take too much. Before getting down to harvesting, look around for more of the same species: Are they abundant, or is yours the only one in sight? If you can't see large amounts of the same kind of plant as you're harvesting, the best course of action is to leave it alone. The reason for this is that you might be harvesting the last plant of its species in the area, and removing it could cause a domino effect that damages the entire surrounding ecosystem. Leave small stands alone or only take a very small amount. Don't harvest from a lone plant, even if you're only pruning: Accidental damage might not become apparent until it's too late.

Finally, the last rule of thumb when determining how much to harvest is to leave everything looking exactly how you've found it. If you step back after harvesting and you can tell that you've been there, you've taken too much.

Legal Concerns

When foraging, it's important to make sure that everything you're doing is legal to avoid getting hit with a nasty fine. Be aware that the Bureau of Land Management (BLM) allows you to pick small amounts of plants on their land for your personal use so long as you don't damage the environment, while the National Park Service does not. Follow the rules of these organizations in order to keep yourself and your party out of trouble.

While you can forage in the wilderness in most cases, as well as on your own property, be very careful that you do not wander onto someone else's privately owned land. Not only could you be confronted by an angry homeowner or dog and potentially fined for trespassing, you don't know the terrain on someone else's property and what hidden dangers could exist there. Don't climb over fences or under gates, and be aware of your surroundings for indicators such as signs or markers that show where private property begins.

Many people who own large forested properties would consider allowing someone to forage there in exchange for a fee or some of the harvest. If you know someone with a property like this, it can be worth it to ask, as many edible plants, such as stinging nettles, are considered nuisances! However, be prepared to hear "No," and respect their decision if they refuse.

There may also be endangered plants in your area that it is illegal to disturb. Harvesting endangered plants is unethical, even where it is legal, as it threatens the entire ecosystem that relies on the plant. A couple examples of endangered plants in the Pacific Northwest are described below.

Endangered Plants in the Pacific Northwest

Gentner's Fritillary (Fritillaria Gentneri)

These beautiful flowers are endangered for a number of reasons, including overharvesting of bulbs by humans.

Identifying Characteristics

Closely related to lilies and similar in appearance, Gentner's fritillary grows in tall stalks. Leaves grow along the stalks in groups of three to five when the flowers are blooming. No leaves are present in juvenile plants. Look also for downwards-tilted flowers with smooth, leaflike petals that are maroon or fuschia with yellow splotches. When the plant is mature enough to flower, they can reach up to 28 inches tall.

Notes

Gentner's fritillary is found throughout Oregon and flowers in the spring, between April and June.

Golden Paintbrush (Castilleja Levisecta)

This flowering plant is mostly endangered because of human encroachment on its native habitat, as well as encroachment by non-native species.

Identifying Characteristics

Golden paintbrush plants are related to snapdragons, and have 5 to 15 unbranched stems per plant. Stems are covered in hairs and may be sticky to the touch. The plants can be up to a foot tall. Leaves grow laterally in groups of one to three from the bottom of the stems to the top, growing more broadly at the bottom of the plants. Golden paintbrush flowers in summer. The flower petals are bright yellow, similar in size and shape to the upper leaves, and turned upwards towards the sky.

Notes

Golden paintbrush grows on prairies and grasslands, particularly in Washington.

Chapter 6:

Foraging With Kids

Many people love to bring their kids along foraging as it's a great way to bond, make memories, and foster teachable moments without relying on screens. Parents have been teaching their children how to identify edible wild plants since prehistoric times, and extending this tradition into the modern day can be deeply rewarding. According to parenting expert Amy McCready, spending quality time with children, even for just a short time, can do wonders for children's development.

In an age where most children's activities take place indoors, foraging is a great way to show kids who are used to spending a lot of time on electronics that the great outdoors can be just as interesting and engaging. Foraging allows them to feel like they're going somewhere and doing something while walking with the family, making it easier to get them interested in exploring the outdoors. Furthermore, getting children outside, exercising and experiencing the world is undoubtedly great for their health, and they'll love contributing to the family's meals by finding edible plants to bring home.

Fig 37. Children in the wilderness. From: Unsplash, by Marcus Wallis, 2018.
https://unsplash.com/photos/MTeZ5FmCGCU Marcus Wallis/Unsplash 2018.

Furthermore, foraging can impart very practical skills and knowledge to children. Harvesting only one part of plants, identifying plants by appearance, and navigating terrain can all help children develop their fine motor skills, mental acuity, and physical fitness. For example, a very young child will quickly pick up harvesting berries without breaking the branches off of the bush. Wild plants can also be used to teach very young children how to count, the names of colors, and words to describe shapes, sizes, and textures. An older child who can handle a knife will learn even more fine-tuned motor skills harvesting mushrooms without disturbing the colony, as well as some basic plant biology by learning the parts of plants and their functions.

Tips and Tricks for Foraging With Children

When taking children out to forage, be sure to talk to them about safety first, and the importance of not eating anything when they haven't confirmed what it is with an adult. Remind them to stay in sight of you, and not to wander off alone. Dress them in bright colors, as this will make them easier for you to keep track of in a forested location. Children should also have their own safety gear, including proper footwear, a high-visibility vest if needed, and gloves. Remember that young children generally need one more layer of clothing than adults are wearing if it's cold, and be aware that they won't be able to walk as far or navigate terrain as well as you can with your much longer legs! Be patient with your children and realistic about their physical abilities.

While most children enjoy walking in the woods and exploring, some might grumble about boredom a little at first. You can make the walking stage of foraging more interesting to them by incorporating little games and competitions that will get their minds working. For example, if you're looking for oyster mushrooms, encourage your kids to look out for them on nearby trees and try to be the first to spot them. You can also encourage them to look out for the bright colors of ripe berries or edible flowers. Older children who are able to learn the names and appearances of different edible plants can take these games up a notch by competing to be the first to spot their favourites.

Giving your kids a little basket or pouch of their own for their finds is a great way to help them feel included. Keep a careful eye on them to make sure they don't eat anything unwashed or unidentified! Older children can start to develop their own foraging toolkits with an age-appropriate folding knife or small shears.

Common Plants to Look Out For

Drawing on our first chapter, we've included some common plants you can find around the Pacific Northwest to forage for with your children. These plants are all very common, and many of them are either sweet-tasting or easily harvestable by children.

Berries: All Kinds!

Berries are some of the best plants to forage for when you're out with kids. Blueberries, blackberries, and raspberries will probably be the most recognizable to children, but they will also love trying berries they might be less familiar with, including mulberries, elderberries, and salmonberries. Berries are excellent things to look for when foraging with kids because their bright colors make them easy to spot, and their sweet taste makes it easier to get kids excited about eating them. Berries can be easily incorporated into pancakes and baked goods, such as the foraged muffins recipe below!

When foraging for berries with kids, remember to provide them with their own gloves so they don't get pricked on thorns! While ideally you should wash your harvest before eating it, when you're out foraging, be sure to reiterate to the younger members of your party not to eat anything if an adult hasn't confirmed what it is first.

Dandelions and Look-alikes

Dandelions are a great thing to look for when foraging with kids for a number of reasons. Firstly, they are completely edible, from the flowers, to the stems, to the leaves and roots. This can give you some peace of mind when you see your kids plucking them by the handful. Secondly, they are not endangered at all, as they are commonly considered weeds or pests, meaning you can collect more of them without stressing about potential harm done to the environment. Thirdly, dandelions can be worked into a number of different foods, from curries and stir frys, to baked goods, to salads (the leaves), and also dandelion tea.

Dandelions also have a number of lookalikes that are also edible, including the agoseris flower.

Chickweed

Chickweed, like dandelions, is commonly thought of as a weed, hence the name. The great thing about that, however, is that it grows practically everywhere, and you won't have to delve deep into the woods to find it. When harvesting chickweed with your kids, make sure that they only pick the newer leaves and tops of the plants, as these parts are digestible raw. Chickweed is better cooked. Use to flavor soups and stews or as a garnish on other dishes!

Recipe: Foraged Muffins

Foraged Muffins

Muffins are great for kids. Not only are they tasty, but you can toss in herbs, fruits, or even shredded vegetables to add an extra kick of vitamins and minerals along with the sugar. Your kids will love adding their foraged harvest to the simple muffin recipe included below. If you don't have muffin pans, you can easily convert this recipe to foraged berry loaf by using bread or cake pans. Just adjust the cooking time to make sure that the finished product is cooked all the way through!

INGREDIENTS (24 MUFFINS)

- 2 cups milk
- 2 eggs
- 1/2 cup plant-based oil (vegetable or canola both work very well)
- 1 cup sugar
- 4 cups of your favourite baking flower (all purpose wheat recommended)
- 1 tbsp baking powder
- Pinch of salt
- Optional: 1 cup mix of foraged berries or fruit (cut up)
- Optional: 2 tbsp foraged herbs (use 1 tbsp if dried)

INSTRUCTIONS

Preheat the oven to 400 degrees Fahrenheit. Grease two muffin pans with butter or oil, or line with paper liners.

In a large mixing bowl, stir together milk, oil, eggs, baking powder, sugar, and salt. Gradually add flour while stirring.

Once a homogenous batter is formed, add in your foraged herbs or berries. Stir a couple of times to distribute evenly, and then stop mixing.

Evenly distribute the batter throughout the muffin pans, and bake for 18 to 20 minutes. Muffins are done when a fork poked into the center comes out clean. Let rest for five minutes and serve.

Chapter 7:

Medicinal Uses for Foraged Plants

Herbalism, or the art and science of using herbs and plants to treat medical ailments, has a history that touches every country on the globe. In the Pacific Northwest, Native American cultures have been using medicinal plants found in the wild for thousands of years, and have developed a wealth of knowledge about wild plants in the region and their uses.

Medicine has many of its roots in herbalism, and many of the compounds we take through pills today had their origins in plants. Medicines usually rely on one or more "active ingredient" that does the 'work' of treating the ailment inside the body through biochemical reactions. Medicinal plants carry these active ingredients naturally, while pharmacological products isolate the active ingredient and carry it in extremely high quantities. Medicinal plants often have a number of unrelated uses because of the wide variety of different compounds that they contain.

This book does not recommend the use of foraged plants as a replacement for medical care. If you have a serious illness requiring treatment, please see a doctor and follow their advice. However, you can use your foraged plants for minor aches, pains, and colds if you prefer something more natural than over-the-counter medications. As herbal medicines can conflict with other medications, consult with your doctor before starting to use herbs to treat minor aches and pains. Never use plants to treat ailments against medical advice, and do not use them if you are pregnant or breastfeeding.

Examples of Medicinal Uses for Wild Plants Found in the Pacific Northwest

Yarrow

Yarrow flowers are extremely medicinal plants and have historically been used to both stop fevers and slow bleeding. Yarrow works as a styptic, by encouraging the formation of scabs. For this reason, yarrow has been applied to minor cuts and abrasions in the form of a mashed poultice or dried powder throughout human history.

A fever is the body's immune response to an infection: It is trying to kill off the bacteria by raising your body temperature. Yarrow works to stop fevers by acting as a diaphoretic, which encourages sweating and opens the pores. Sweating is one of our body's natural ways of cooling down, as evaporating sweat cools the skin.

These are only two of the many functions of yarrow. Look in the list below for some of its other potential uses!

Indian Pipe

Also known as ghost plant, this striking and mysterious plant has been used as a pain reliever, especially to relieve muscle aches from colds and flus. Indian pipe works as a nervine, which is a herbal compound that acts on the nervous system, usually with a calming effect. It can be drunk as an infusion for this purpose, or otherwise placed on a bruise or sore muscle as a tincture.

The soothing effects of Indian pipe also make it a viable option as a sedative, to help relieve insomnia. If pain is keeping you up from sleep, Indian pipe could be a viable option.

Medicinal Uses of Wild Plants in the Pacific Northwest

Here, common minor ailments are listed with medicinal plants commonly used to treat them. The plants included in this list have profiles in this book, helping you to look for them the next time you go foraging. There are numerous other guides out there with more comprehensive lists of medicinal plants and their potential uses. While infusions are the most common way of delivering the active ingredient of medicinal foraged plants, it's worth it to do some research to determine the best delivery method of a plant before using it.

Sore Throat

- Self heal

- Yarrow

- Mulberry

- Knotweed

Aches and Pains

- Yarrow

- Indian pipe

- Wild chamomile

- Devil's club

- Russian olive

Runny Nose/Colds

- Goldenrod

- Yarrow

- Indian pipe

- Knotweed

Constipation

- Dandelion

- Watercress

- Agoseris

- Miner's lettuce

- Bedstraw

Insomnia

- Wild chamomile

- Dandelion

- Sea milkwort

- Indian pipe

Fever

- Yarrow

- Indian pipe

- Wild chamomile

- Self heal

Arthritis

- Watercress

- Indian pipe

- Mulberry

- Devil's club

- Russian olive

Recipes: Teas to Feel Better

Both of the recipes below make about two cups of dried tea; the perfect size to keep in a regular mason jar. To infuse, spoon a regular tablespoon into a tea bag or infuser, place in a mug, and cover with hot water. Do not use boiling water: This will burn the dried leaves in the mixture. Teas should steep for up to 10 minutes.

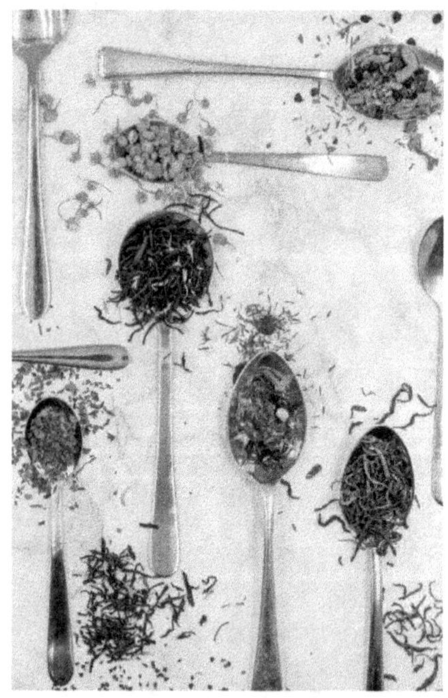

Fig 38. Assorted teas. From: Unsplash, by Alice Pasqual, 2019. https://unsplash.com/photos/xdD-x2Y2SPI Copyright Alice Pasqual/Unsplash 2019.

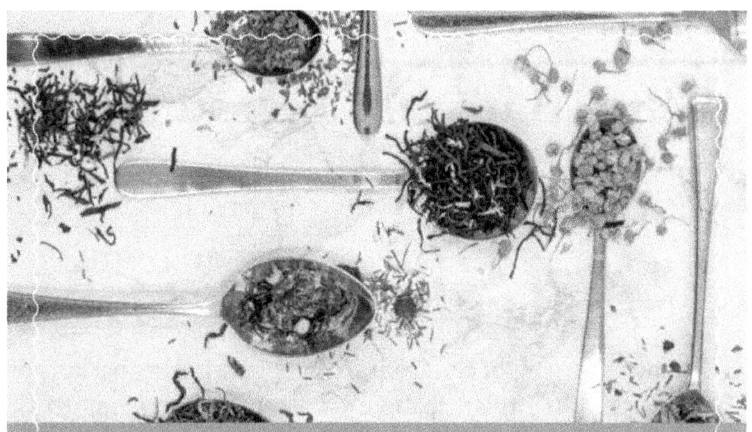

Teas to Feel Better

Calm-Down Tea

By mixing wild chamomile and sea milkwort, this tea is bound to get you ready to drift off into a restful sleep. Blackberries, salmonberries, and mulberries hide the bitter taste of sea milkwort with their tart, sweet flavors. Only consume before bedtime, and avoid operating heavy machinery after drinking.

INGREDIENTS

- ¾ cup dried wild chamomile/pineapple weed
- ½ cup dried sea milkwort rhizome
- ¼ cup dried blackberries
- ¼ cup dried mulberries
- ¼ cup dried salmonberries

Tea for a Bad Cold

The plants included in this tea are known to help with sore throats and coughs. The flavoring comes from sweet blueberries and raspberries, allowing you to enjoy this soothing and calming medicinal blend without the bitterness from the medicinal plants.

INGREDIENTS

- ½ cup dried self heal
- ½ cup dried false Solomon's seal
- ¼ cup dried bittercress
- ½ cup dried blueberries
- ¼ cup dried raspberries

Chapter 8:

Water Bath and Pressure Canning

When you get back from foraging with a basket or backpack full of plants, there's no way you're going to be able to eat your whole harvest all at once! Luckily, there's a vast range of different methods for preserving your harvests so you can eat them at your leisure, and some, like jam-making, can make them even tastier! Some of these methods are newer and require a bit of extra technology, while others have been practiced for thousands of years and can be done mostly with things you find around your kitchen. Learning two or three of these methods, most of which are very simple, gives you the tools you need to stock your pantry with jars of delicious foraged plants that you can whip out at any time to spice up a meal. Plus, homemade jams, preserves, and pickles all make great additions to gifts during the holidays!

Water Bath Canning

Canning vegetables is one of the most common ways to preserve them, and has been practiced worldwide by a vast range of cultures for an even wider range of foods. Not only is canning an extremely convenient way to prevent foods from going bad, it's the basis of two of the other processes described in the following chapter!

Equipment for Water Bath Canning

While dedicated appliances for water bath canning exist, recall that canning has been a common food preservation method for long before their invention. This book provides a very simple and low-tech method for canning foods, though investing in higher-tech equipment is perfectly fine if that's what you prefer!

Safety note: water bath canning is only suitable for acidic food mixtures. In order to prevent your food from becoming unsafe to eat, double check that your ingredients are safe for water bath canning before proceeding. If you want to can non-acidic vegetables or other foods, you do need to invest in a pressure canner to do this. More information on pressure canning is provided below.

In order to properly use a hot water bath to seal cans, or jars, of food, you need to find a large, tall pot, like a stockpot. Many people have a suitable pot somewhere in their kitchen, while others might need to invest. The pot should be big enough that you can completely submerge the cans you're using without filling it to a dangerous level. Remember, you're going to be working with boiling water, so pay attention to safety! You'll also need a set of tongs that are large enough to comfortably reach into the water in the pot and grab out the mason jars, or purchase "jar lifters" which are metal tongs with heads designed for this purpose. You may also choose to wear gloves even while you do this, to prevent burns from accidental splashes. You will also need a wooden spoon, spatula, chopstick, or other utensil to manipulate the cans without touching them. Pretty much all of these items can be found in your kitchen drawers and cabinets!

Some things, however, you're more likely to have to purchase before getting started. A rack to put inside the pot, in order to keep the cans still, is recommended to can food properly and safely, though not all guides include them. Without a rack, evaporating air would cause the cans to knock against each other, and possibly break. You don't want to be fishing broken glass and bits of food out of the bottom of a pot! A canning funnel is also recommended. This will help you get food into the canning jar without dirtying the rims, which can make it harder for a correct seal to form.

Canning jars (also simply called 'cans') are glass jars with two-piece lids. This type of lid, where a metal plate goes on top of the jar and is secured by a metal ring that is screwed on, is essential to canning safely as this allows the formation of an airtight seal. It's important that your lids are the correct size for the cans or they won't seal properly.

Finally, you need damp, clean paper towels to moisten the can rims, and you're good to go!

Sanitizing Your Jars

Before you start filling canning jars with food, it's important to make sure your jars are sterile. This kills off unwanted bacteria that would allow your food to decompose and become unsafe.

One occasional exception to this rule is if your particular recipe calls for the jars to be boiled for more than 10 minutes. This is thought to provide enough heat to kill bacteria without sanitizing the jars separately. Pressure canners also provide enough heat to kill bacteria during the regular canning process. Still, it's better to be safe than sorry, and sterilizing your jars regardless can help assure you that your food will be safe to eat when you open the cans. If you are not using a pressure canner, and your recipe instructs you to boil your canning jars for less than 10 minutes, always, always sanitize them first!

While a variety of methods circulate on the internet, submerging cans in boiling water is the only USDA-approved method of sterilizing them. If you have a boiling water canner, specific instructions for your appliance are likely found in the instruction manual. Any pot suitable for water bath canning (big enough to be fitted with a rack and still have room to cover the jars with water by a couple of inches) can also be used to sterilize jars. This will probably be the same pot you do your canning in!

To sanitize your jars, set up your large pot and rack on the stove, but do not fill with water or turn on the heat yet. Arrange the jars to be sanitized on the rack, with their mouths facing the opening of the pot. Fill the pot with hot (but not boiling) water so that the cans are covered by an inch of water. If your pot is large enough, there will be at least one inch of space between the surface of the water and the top of the pot. Turn the heat up to high and boil the jars for at least 10 minutes before turning off the heat. The water will stay sterile for an hour as it cools, so you can leave your jars there while you prepare the food to be canned. As always, using tongs to lift your jars out is an important way to protect yourself from burns.

Note: the altitude you live at affects the boiling temperature of water, and people living in more elevated regions need to boil their jars longer to make up for this. A quick Google search can let you know the altitude you live at, and a simple rule of thumb is to start by boiling jars for 10 minutes, add one minute of boiling time for every 1000 feet above sea level. If you're unsure, it's better to opt for a longer boiling period.

Canning requires two-piece style lids in order to work properly. This comes with a round lid that goes on top of the jar and a ring that screws on to hold it in place. Lids should not be reused (and can be bought in bulk), but rings can be if they are sanitized properly. In order to sanitize your two piece jar lids, place them into hot, simmering water for 10 minutes and remove with tongs. Don't let this water get to boiling as the extreme heat can cause the metal lids to warp, allowing air into your cans that would let your food start to decompose.

Raw Packing and Hot Packing

Now that your jars are clean and sterile, it's time to get down to the canning! There are two ways to arrange the food inside the cans for safe results. These are known as raw packing and hot packing. Both of these methods are acceptable ways to can food, but you may decide to use one or the other depending on what equipment you have available and what kind of canning you're doing. Generally, people using the water bath canning method use hot packing, but both techniques will be described here.

Raw packing, also known as cold packing, is more appropriate for pressure canning as it does not heat the food in advance, though occasionally people use this method for water bath canning projects as well. To raw pack food, simply cut up the plants and put them in the jar covered with the water, syrup, or other liquid you're using to preserve them. Be sure that there's at least a quarter inch of room between the surface of the food and the lid of the jar.

Hot packing is most commonly used for water bath canning and ensures that food remains safe to eat in the can over time. It does this by removing air from the food (preventing it from decomposing), and also causing more of a vacuum to exist inside the jars. Hot packing also causes food to shrink, making it possible to pack more into each can. Many people also feel that hot packing allows food to keep its color longer, making it more aesthetically pleasing and appetizing. When food is hot-packed, it is simmered on the stove together or separately with the liquid it is being preserved in. You can see examples of hot-packing in the following chapter, which instructs on different ways to preserve food.

Instructions for Water Bath Canning

Before sanitizing jars and lids, inspect them for damage or imperfections. Chipped, fractured, or otherwise defective cans are unsafe to use and should be discarded before you begin.

Once your jars are cleared, use the raw or hot packing procedure to fill them according to your recipe. Work quickly, but don't rush, especially if you're using boiling water for the hot packing method. Put the lids on the jars and screw on the rings until they are snug, but not as tight as they can go. You want the rings to be secure, but not so tight that leftover air can't seep out during the canning process.

Now that the jars of food are ready, it's time to start your water bath. Put your large pot on the stove and place the canning rack inside. Fill with water so that the surface level would be at least one inch above the surface of the jars and bring to a boil on high heat. Using tongs, place the jars upright on the rack, being careful not to tip them as you don't want food touching the rims. If there's not enough water to fully cover the jars, add more hot water from a kettle. You can turn down the heat a little if the water is boiling over, as long as it stays at a roiling boil. Cover the pot and start the timer. Depending on what you're canning, the time required in the boiling water will vary, so be sure to double-check the recipe you're using.

Once the timer goes off, turn off the heat and wait for the boiling water to calm down, a minimum of five minutes. Remove the pot lid, being careful not to scald your face or hands on the escaping steam. Using tongs, remove the jars from the water (without tilting them) and place them on a wire rack or dish towel on the counter. Don't disturb the jars for at least 12 hours. Leaving the jars alone will allow the food inside to cool and settle without touching the rim or lid, which can interfere with the all-important seal.

To be sure that the lids have formed a proper seal, press down on them with your finger after the 12 hour period. If the lids don't move or wiggle under pressure, a proper seal has been formed. If any jars have a defective seal, you can put them in the fridge and consume their contents over the next few days. For the jars that are sealed properly, you can safely move them to the pantry to enjoy at your leisure. Most canned foods still have an expiry date, so check your recipe for this to be sure. You can write the expiry dates of canned food on the lids with Sharpie or another permanent marker.

Pressure Canning

Pressure canners are specially-made pots that encourage the buildup of pressure inside to process jars of food. They have a vent to allow you to release steam to regulate the pressure. Pressure canners come with their own instruction guides based on their design, so if the manual that came with your pressure canner conflicts with the advice here, it's best to follow the package instructions.

To start the pressure canning process, add the rack to the pot, followed by water. While the amount varies depending on the pressure canner, it is generally a smaller amount of water than with water bath canning, often just three inches from the bottom of the canner. For recipes that require longer periods in the pressure canner (40 minutes or more) add more water as more will be lost during the process.

If you are hot-packing your food, feel free to turn the stove on high now. If you're raw-packing, don't turn on the stove yet or you'll risk cracking the jars. In this case, wait until the jars are in the canner to turn up the heat. If you're raw-packing, you may decide to leave more room, as the food will float in the water inside the jars.

Using tongs, place the jars on the rack inside the pressure canner and put on the lid, securing it according to package instructions. Turn up the heat if you haven't already. There is a switch or dial on the top of the pressure canning lid, which you can use to vent steam. You'll know you've reached a roiling boil when a lot of steam starts escaping the canner's vents. It's important to have this open at first, usually for a period of 10 minutes, though it's important to refer to your canner's instructions as some models require a different length of time. After that time, shut the vent, being careful not to scald yourself on the steam. Pressure will now start building up inside the canner and you can check the pressure level using the meter on the front of the pot. When the level of pressure recommended by your canner's manual is attained, set a timer for however long the recipe requires. Keep an eye on the canner and adjust the vents if the pressure grows too high. However, if the pressure gets too low, turn up the heat to adjust it and restart the timer. The canner needs to be at the specified level of pressure during the entire process to ensure the food is safe for consumption.

At the end of the process, turn off the heat and let the canner cool down and depressurize itself for at least five minutes before re-opening the vent. If you hear a hiss, don't remove the lid. Stop and wait for the canner to fully depressurize to avoid being injured.

Slowly lift off the lid so that the steam escapes on the side away from your face. Now your cans are ready to come out. Be sure to use tongs! Just like with water bath canning, let them stand undisturbed for at least 12 hours to cool and settle before moving them to the pantry.

Chapter 9

Ways to Preserve Your Harvest

Jams, Jellies, and Preserves

What's the difference between jams, jellies, and preserves? While many people conflate them, these are actually three different types of preserved fruit with different processes for making them. Jams consist of crushed fruit mixed with sugar and pectin, a carbohydrate that appears naturally in a number of plants. Jam often contains seeds or bits of fruit and has a distinct texture. Jelly, on the other hand, is sugar and pectin mixed with fruit juice, and comes out smooth without the texture or 'bits' found in jam. Preserves forgo the crushing or juicing process entirely: Fruits or berries are simply chopped up and preserved in syrup.

Pectin can be purchased in most grocery stores. Depending on what fruit you're using, you may be able to forgo purchased pectin or use a smaller amount because of the high pectin content in the fruit itself. As a general rule of thumb, firm or under-ripe fruits and berries with a tart or sour flavour have a higher amount of pectin.

Safety note: regardless of whether your recipe requires you to sterilize the jars beforehand, make sure they are clean and hot when you pour hot mixtures into them. This will prevent them from cracking due to heat. A low-effort way to do this is by putting them through a cycle in the dishwater right before you use them.

Making Jams

Jam is the most common type of preserved fruit, and the sky's the limit regarding what kind of berries you can use. While strawberry, blueberry, and raspberry are the most classic flavors, you can really wow your family or your guests by bringing out a homemade jam made from your foraging harvests.

In order to make jam safely and properly, make sure that your berries are as clean as possible by washing them in cool water. Don't allow the fruit to soak in water because this will make your jam waterier than it should be. Once the fruit is clean, lay out clean paper towels on the counter and spread the fruit out on top to dry.

While added sugar is part of most jam recipes, choosing ripe berries will ensure your jam is as naturally sweet as possible. Go through your berries and remove any that are rotten or overripe, and then remove any leaves, flowers, or stems that might still be stuck to them. If you're using larger fruits, now is the time to cut them up, but if you only have berries, you can skip that step. Crush the fruits by mashing them through a colander into a bowl, or use a food mill if you have one. You'll get sticky hands during this step, so it helps to have water on hand to rinse them!

The USDA guide to safe jam-making does not recommend added water for making jam from ripe berries, but some recipes do call for water, so check the one you're using to make sure. In most cases, the crushed fruit is placed in a saucepan on the stove with added sugar, and simmered while stirring constantly. While the amount of sugar varies per recipe, it's usually about ¾ to 1 cup per cup of crushed fruit. If you are using a sweet type of berry and added pectin is required, either use the amount of pectin recommended for your specific fruit on the package, or add two tablespoons of lemon juice at this step.

Continue stirring while your jam simmers. Once the mixture starts to thicken, spoon a small amount onto a plate or tray and place it in the freezer for three to four minutes. Take it out and poke it with your finger or the back of a spoon. If it has formed a gelatinous mass that wrinkles under pressure, it's done!

Ladle the jam mixture into clean, hot jars with moistened rims, using a wide-mouthed canning funnel, and proceed with the water bath canning process.

Making Jellies

In order to make jelly properly, there's a small amount of equipment needed, outside of what you will use to can the jelly at the end. You will need a saucepan, spoon, and colander or sieve, as well as cheesecloth to tightly strain the juice you'll be extracting.

When you're out foraging, try to gather a mix of ripe and under-ripe berries, as under-ripe berries will be higher in pectin. As some species of berries are unsafe to eat while under-ripe, double check that it's safe to use the species you've found before proceeding. The USDA guide to home canning suggests a three to one ratio of ripe to under-ripe berries for homemade jelly, if you don't want to add commercial pectin. For species of berry or fruit that do require commercial pectin (such as blueberries, raspberries, salmonberries, or other sweeter varieties), follow the amount listed on the recipe you're using as this varies by species. The packaging of many brands of store-bought pectin sometimes also indicates how much is required for different fruits and berries. Pectin can also be added by mixing in one to two tsp of lemon juice per cup of fruit juice.

The first step of making jelly is juicing your foraged fruit. You can do this by placing them in a saucepan, covering them with water, and simmering them until soft, usually for approximately 20 minutes. The amount of water and simmering time required varies by fruit species. Including peels and cores in the pan along with the flesh of the fruit for juice allows you to extract more pectin, ensuring you'll get the gelatinous texture you're looking for in your finished jelly. Once the fruit is soft, strain it through a colander followed by cheesecloth to get all the unwanted 'bits' out. You can expect roughly a cup of juice per pound of fruit used. This differs from regular juicing by crushing the fruit, as it prevents pulp, seeds, or any other bits from ending up in the juice.

To strain through cheesecloth, make a 'bag' out of the cloth and put the simmered fruit inside, allowing it to drip through into a bowl or other receptacle. Be sure not to poke or squeeze the cheesecloth during this process, even if the juice seems to be dripping out slowly! This allows some smaller chunks to escape, ruining the smooth texture of the jelly. Place the cheesecloth in a colander with something underneath to collect the juice, and use this time to prepare the rest of your equipment and measure out your sugar and other flavourings.

You'll need to add sugar, which can be regular granulated sugar, to most jellies to make them come out properly. While the amount varies according to recipe, this is usually ¾ cup to 1 cup per cup of fruit juice. Some recipes also call for added water.

Mix the sugar, juice, and water, lemon juice or commercial pectin (if needed) in a saucepan and heat to boiling, stirring constantly. You can use a cool metal spoon to check if the jelly is done. Under-done jelly will drip off of your spoon in droplets, but once you lift your spoon and see the jelly starting to form two large drops or a sheet as it slowly pours off, you know you've reached the jelly-ing point.

Remove jelly from heat and, using a ladle, distribute it to clean, hot canning jars with moistened rims, making sure there's at least a ¼ inch of room between the jelly and the lid of the cans. Screw on lids and proceed with the water bath canning process.

Making Preserves

When you make preserves, you'll be following much of the same procedure as when you make jam or jelly. The difference is with preserves, you won't be adding pectin to make the mixture more gelatinous, but instead will be canning them in a sugary liquid. You will also not be crushing or juicing your fruit or berries, but simply cutting them up. These will soften during the simmering process.

Choose ripe fruits and berries for your preserves and wash thoroughly. Cut up larger fruit into small pieces, but do not crush: You want the fruit to maintain a little bit of structural integrity!

The liquid you use to can your preserves can be water with added sugar, syrup, juice, or even jam! The specific liquid used, and the ratio between the liquid and the fruit, varies by recipe. This is where you can really let your creativity shine and get more foraged foods into the mix, by creating whatever unique combinations of flavors you can come up with!

Place the crushed fruit in a saucepan with the liquid, bring to a simmer, and cook until softened. Ladle the preserves into clean, hot, canning jars with moistened lids. As with jam and jelly, be sure that there's ¼ inch of headspace when you ladle the preserves into your jars. Proceed with the water bath canning process.

Pickling and Fermenting

Pickling and fermenting are two very similar processes that are often conflated, so what's the difference between them? While both processes involve soaking vegetables in an acidic solution, the difference lies in where that acid comes from. When you pickle vegetables, you add the acid by hand at the beginning of the process, which preserves the food. On the flip side, fermentation requires a little extra help from the natural bacteria present in our food. When a vegetable rots or decomposes normally, bacteria feed on the sugars present in the plant, gradually breaking it down over time. However, when there is no oxygen available, the bacteria can't consume the sugars in the same way, turning instead to a different chemical reaction that produces lactic acid as a byproduct. With nowhere to drain away, this lactic acid builds up and provides the acid needed to preserve the food. Therefore, while these processes are very similar, they produce results with somewhat different tastes and textures.

Making Pickles

Just like with the methods of preserving fruit above, preserving pickles starts with a clean canning jar, which has been sterilized in boiling water if necessary, depending on your recipe. You will also need your foraging harvest, of course, as well as something to provide the acid. This usually takes the form of vinegar. Looking at your kitchen cupboard, you might have a couple kinds of vinegar on hand, and which one you use can affect the flavor of the final product. For example, your regular white vinegar produces a very sharp, zingy flavor, while apple cider vinegar will make your pickles come out milder and sweeter. You may also add flavorings to your pickling mixture, such as hot peppers, peppercorns, dill, garlic, or other herbs and spices. This is a great way to incorporate more of your foraged harvest!

Pickling salt is also an important part of the pickling process, and may not be found in your cupboard. Using regular table salt can throw off the flavor of the finished product, so investing in pickling salt before you get started is definitely worth it!

To get started pickling, fill a large bowl with your foraged vegetables (cut up to fit in the jars if necessary), and pickling salt in an amount called for by your recipe. Cover the bowl in saran wrap, aluminum foil, or a clean dishcloth, and leave undisturbed for three hours. You can use this time to sterilize your canning jars, prepare your canning pot, and make room in the kitchen for the rest of the process.

Next, scrape the vegetable and salt mixture into a saucepan, and add water, vinegar, and any other flavorings in accordance with your recipe. Bring to a lively simmer and stir occasionally to ensure everything is evenly distributed. While simmer time varies depending on recipe, it usually falls around approximately five minutes.

Ladle the pickle mixture into clean, hot canning jars with moistened rims, and screw the lid on, ensuring you leave at least a quarter inch of room so that the pickling mixture does not touch the lid. Proceed with your regular water bath canning process, store, and enjoy!

Fermenting Your Foraged Foods

Fermenting food takes a little longer than the other methods described in this guide, as instead of canning your food right after boiling, you'll need to wait for nature to take its course and preserve the food for you.

As bacteria are essential to the fermenting process, it's essential to make sure you only have the bacteria you want in the fermenting crock with your food. In order to prevent the buildup of harmful bacteria, wash all of your food and equipment thoroughly. For safety reasons, the USDA strongly recommends starting the fermenting process within 24 hours of harvest so that the food doesn't start to break down before you start.

While there are different methods for fermenting, the easiest and most efficient requires the use of a fermenting crock, which is a stone or ceramic vessel that helps you achieve the zero-oxygen conditions required for fermenting food properly and safely. While this is a bit of an investment in comparison to the other equipment described in this guide, it's one you definitely won't regret once you start using it to make delicious, tangy fermented snacks from your foraging harvests!

There are a couple different types of fermenting crocks. The first is the open fermenting crock, which looks like a simple stone or ceramic pot, sometimes with a lid. While this seems very odd as fermentation requires no oxygen to be present with the food during the process, these vessels are ingeniously designed to achieve just that. Since food is covered by brine during fermentation, open fermenting crocks come with weights that hold the food down under the brine, away from air. If you bought your open fermenting crock secondhand and didn't receive a weight with it, you can use any sanitized, heavy item you can find in your kitchen or around the house, as long as you're okay with it smelling like fermented food afterwards! During the fermenting process, you can cover your open fermenting crock with the accompanying lid or with a clean dishcloth to keep flies from getting to the food.

The second most popular type of fermenting crock is a water-sealed crock. This more modern incarnation of the fermenting crock has a lip on the inside that you fill with plain water, along with a specially fitted lid that goes on top. The design of these crocks allows carbon dioxide from the fermenting process to escape through the water bubble, but stops air from getting in. While these are more expensive than open crocks, there is a lower chance of anything accidentally going wrong with the process, so some people prefer them over their simpler cousins.

To get started fermenting, you need clean, recently harvested foraged foods, as well as water and salt to make brine, as well as any flavorings you'll want to add to the brine. Just like with pickling, you're only limited by your imagination for what these flavorings can be, so don't be afraid to experiment!

Make sure your fermenting crock is washed thoroughly with hot, soapy water. If you're using an open crock with weights, soak these in water before use. This will stop them soaking up the brine and taking on a smell.

The next step is to make the brine and mix in the food to be fermented. Make sure your food is clean, and then chop or shred it as desired. If your food has a high water content, as many plant shoots do, you can make a briny mixture by mixing it with a few tablespoons of sea salt and mashing it, while other recipes call for making a brine with salt and water. Check your recipe to see if added water is necessary before continuing, but remember that the most important thing is for the food in the fermenting crock to be completely covered.

Add the veggies, any herbs and spices, and the brine to the fermenting crock. If bits are poking out of the surface of the brine, you need more water, and be sure to balance this with additional salt. Cover the crock according to package instructions and leave in a place it will not be disturbed. If you're using an open crock, you might have to skim some yeast or bubbles off the top on occasion, but other than that, natural bacteria do the rest of the work for you! Some fermenting crocks bubble over during this process, spilling a small amount of brine onto the counter: Place your crock on top of a tray or baking sheet to keep this contained.

How long the fermenting process takes depends on your recipe and the food involved, but your fermented food will be ready between one to two weeks. If you want a very intense flavor, you can leave it longer. You can keep fermented foods in the fridge for a few days, but otherwise, ladle it into clean canning jars with moistened rims, screw on the lids, and start the water bath canning process.

Dried Foods

Drying foods is a very different process from canning them, but this is another great way to ensure that your food stays good over time. Dried plants can be stored very densely in whichever container is convenient, so long as they're in a cool, dry, place, making it a great way to save room in your pantry. Furthermore, drying mushrooms is actually one of the most common ways to store them over time as you can return most of the moisture to mushrooms by soaking them in water, a process known as reconstitution. Dried leaves, herbs, and berries can all become part of herbal teas, or mixed with your favourite black or green tea if you prefer a kick of caffeine: Either way, drying out foraged plants allows you to make your own unique blends to suit your tastes! Furthermore, drying herbs can allow you to keep them around for a long time, ready to be used to add flavor to dishes no matter the season.

Drying Herbs

There are plenty of advantages to drying out herbs at home, rather than buying them at the store: You know that these herbs are fresh and full of flavor and haven't been sitting on a shelf for months! Furthermore, a number of herbs that are favourites for cooking and teas, such as chamomile, have wild varieties growing up and down the Pacific Northwest. Collecting and drying out foraged harvest at home means you'll always have these delicious flavors at your fingertips. Drying your herb harvests allows you to forage more ethically as well by cutting back on waste and allowing you to keep herbs around until you're ready to use them. It also cuts back on the use of space, as drying herbs have a smaller volume than fresh. Finally, dried herbs pack more of a flavor punch than fresh, and you can use smaller quantities in recipes with the same results.

While hanging up herbs to dry is simple and easy, there are a couple things to remember in order to get the best results. When you divide your foraged herbs into bundles, make sure that you don't make them too thick, as this prevents air from getting at the stalks in the middle. A one-inch diameter should be the maximum. You also want to make sure that your herbs are hanging in a dry room so that moisture in the air does not cause mold to grow. Finally, you should use a rubber band, not string or tape, to hold the herb bundles together. The reason for this was mentioned above: Dried herbs have a smaller volume than larger herbs, and you don't want them to fall out of the bundle as they dry. Twisting a rubber band tightly around the bundle will allow it to contract with the herbs. You can also easily adjust a rubber band if you notice it's becoming loose.

Different species of herb take different lengths of time to dry because of differences in water and oil content, and humidity in the air can also affect the time needed. Most herbs dry out in approximately a week. You'll know that your herbs are done when you can easily crumple them into pieces with your fingers and they are totally dry to the touch. They should appear significantly shrunken compared to fresh herbs, and their color will be much duller and darker. At this stage, you should be able to take them down, crumple them by hand or with a food mill, and add to jars.

What if you don't have the space to hang herbs up for a week? An alternative method would be to spread out parchment paper on a cookie sheet and lay the herbs out to dry on top. This method works best for types of herbs with wide, flat leaves. If you go this way, make sure that the herbs on the tray aren't touching each other. Place them in a low-traffic area where there's no breeze to disturb them (not in front of the window!) and out of reach of pets and children. Possible locations could be on top of a cupboard or refrigerator.

Drying Foraged Plants in the Oven

As drying out fruits, vegetables, and mushrooms is so convenient for preventing food waste and creating a vast range of delicious snacks, it's no wonder that appliances were invented to do just that. A dehydrator is a small appliance that allows you to dry meat and vegetables at low heat for a specified period of time. However, you don't need a dehydrator to effectively dry food!

In the section below, we'll cover how to dry a variety of foraged foods in the oven you have at home! Be aware that drying can take several hours depending on the species, and that your oven will be out of commission during that time, and be sure to plan your day accordingly.

Note: Some ovens have a minimum setting of 170 degrees Fahrenheit, while the recommended temperatures for drying foods are usually below this. If this is the minimum setting of your oven, don't worry: Just make sure that you slice your foods thinner to make sure they dry all the way through, and check up on them as they dry to be sure they don't burn.

Mushrooms

Drying is probably the most popular way to preserve mushrooms of all time, as these delicious fungi easily regain moisture by reconstituting. Reconstituted mushrooms are great in soups, stews, curries, or any other cooked meal. Some people even say that mushrooms that have been dried are more flavourful than their fresh counterparts. Furthermore, the water you use to soak the dried mushrooms takes on their earthy flavor and is referred to by some chefs as "liquid gold." Try using this as a delicious mushroom stock for soup!

Before beginning to dry them, go through your mushrooms, remove any that have gone bad, and cut off any rotten parts. If a mushroom is soft or slimy, throw it out. Give your fresh mushrooms a thorough wash with cold water to remove any dirt, bugs, or other debris. Once they're clean, spread them out on a paper towel to dry. It's essential that the mushrooms are not wet when they go into the oven or they'll cook instead of dehydrating. Blot them firmly with paper towels if you don't have time to wait for them to air-dry.

Your oven needs to be set at a very low temperature for the drying process to work properly. 150 degrees Fahrenheit is recommended for most mushrooms. Drying out mushrooms too fast will cause them to have a dried exterior but moisture inside, allowing them to get moldy and become unsafe to eat despite your efforts.

While the oven is preheating, prepare a cookie sheet with a parchment paper or cheesecloth lining. Chop up the fresh mushrooms if desired: smaller Slices will dry more quickly and easily than large chunks. Spread them out evenly on the tray so they are not touching each other and pop them in the oven, setting a timer for 30 minutes.

Once the timer goes off, take out the mushrooms and turn them over using a spatula or tongs, then put them back in. You'll have to repeat this every half hour until the mushrooms are dry. The whole process can take one to three hours in total, depending on the thickness of the mushroom slices.

When the mushrooms are completely dry, take the tray out of the oven and let them cool completely. This allows them to finish crisping up without sticking together. You can store dried mushrooms in a labelled jar in a cool dry place for several months, but they're best within one month of drying.

To restore moisture to mushrooms, place a few handfuls in a mixing bowl and cover with boiling water. They'll be ready to use in 20 to 30 minutes, plus you'll have a convenient bowl of mushroom stock as well!

Fruits and Vegetables

Drying fruits and vegetables in the oven works mostly in the same way as drying mushrooms. Once again, you want your oven to be at a very low setting, around 140 degrees Fahrenheit. Using the convection setting of your oven can cut down on the time it takes fruits and vegetables to dry, but you can still proceed if your oven doesn't have it.

Wash everything thoroughly, and cut larger fruits and vegetables into thinner slices.

Thicker vegetables need to be lightly blanched before drying, as this allows them to dry through completely. This can be most easily done in the microwave. Once your vegetables have been cut up, place them in a microwave-safe bowl with ¼ cup of water to each pound of vegetables, and microwave on high for three ot four minutes. Stir and poke with a fork, being careful not to scald yourself on the steam. If they aren't tender yet, add a little more water and microwave another one to two minutes.

Fruit, on the other hand, needs to be conditioned before drying. If your fruit has a thick skin, you need to crack the skin so that it allows the inside of the fruit to dry. Dip fruit in boiling water for 30 to 60 seconds, followed by ice water for 30 to 60 seconds. You can make a bag out of cheesecloth to hold the fruit and lower them into the water to avoid scalding your hand. Next, place all fruit (even those that didn't need their skins cracked) in cups of lemon or lime juice for 15 to 30 minutes. This will help kill off any mold or bacteria, ensuring that your dried fruit stays safe to eat. Finally, mix the fruit into a mixing bowl of sugar and allow to sit for one hour, which makes sure that your dried fruit is chewy and retains its sweetness. You can forgo this step if you're planning to use your dried fruit in baked goods or teas, but it's best to include it if you're going to eat them in a salad or trail mix.

Lay your fruits and vegetables out on a tray with a parchment paper lining and place into the oven. Drying fruits and vegetables takes much longer than mushrooms, sometimes up to seven or eight hours depending on the species of plant and the thickness they were cut to. Expect a drying time of four to six hours if you're using your oven's convection setting.

Chapter 10

Recipes With Foraged Plants

Breakfast: Watercress Dandelion Scramble

Watercress Dandelion Scramble

INGREDIENTS (15 MINUTES, SERVES 2):

- 4 large eggs
- 2 tbsp olive oil or margarine
- 2 cloves garlic
- 1 white onion, chopped
- 1 tomato, finely chopped
- ½ tbsp dried parsley
- 2 handfuls watercress
- 1 handful dandelion or agoseris leaves
- Salt and pepper to taste

INSTRUCTIONS:

Melt margarine or heat olive oil in a large pan over medium heat. Chop onions and garlic, and cook in the hot oil until translucent and fragrant.

Chop tomato, parsley, watercress, and dandelion leaves. Add tomato to the pan and cook until sizzling.

Crack eggs into a bowl and whisk until a smooth liquid is formed. Pour over the tomatoes and onions, stirring continuously to scramble and mix.

Add parsley, watercress, and dandelion leaves, and continue stirring.

Scramble is done when pieces split easily when poked with a spatula and are cooked on the inside, about six to seven minutes after adding the eggs.

Wild Mushroom Dishes

Inspired by the excellent stuffed morels recipe by Holley at The Primal Desire (The Primal Desire, 2020).

INGREDIENTS (1 HOUR, SERVES 2):

- ½ pound morels
- ½ cup miner's lettuce
- ½ cup young stinging nettle leaves
- 2 cloves garlic
- 1 cup ricotta cheese
- 1 small onion
- 2 tbsp butter
- Salt and pepper to taste

INSTRUCTIONS:

Preheat the oven to 350 degrees Fahrenheit. While chopping and preparing other ingredients, soak morels in saltwater for at least 15 minutes.

Place miner's lettuce, stinging nettle leaves, garlic, cheese, and onion in a blender. Using the pulse setting, process until a chunky mixture is formed.

Stuff the morels with the mixture using clean hands or a wooden spoon. A plastic bag with one corner cut off can be used as a funnel to streamline this process.

Place stuffed morels on a cookie sheet with a parchment paper lining.

Melt butter in the microwave in a microwave-safe container, and drizzle evenly over the morels. Season generously with salt and pepper.

Bake for 30 to 40 minutes until the ridges of the morels are thoroughly browned.

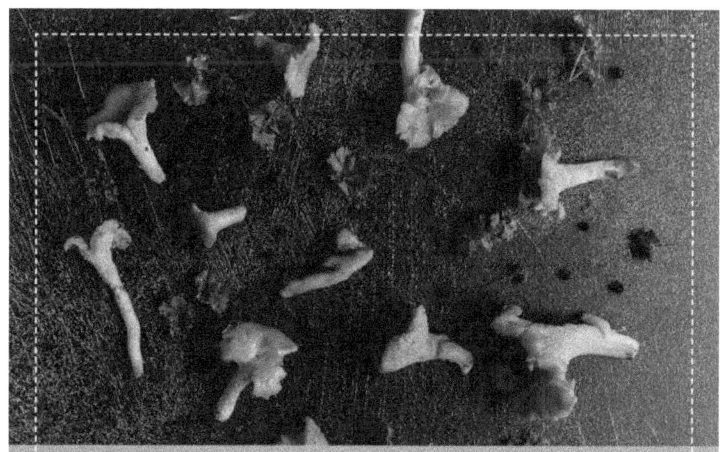

Roasted Pacific Golden Chanterelle with Herbs

INGREDIENTS (90 MINUTES, SERVES 2)

- 1 pound Pacific golden chanterelles, washed and chopped
- 1 tbsp olive oil
- 1 tsp dried parsley
- 1 tsp dried rosemary
- 1 tsp dried thyme
- Salt and pepper to taste

INSTRUCTIONS

Preheat the oven to 430 degrees Fahrenheit. Roughly chop the Pacific golden chanterelles, and toss with olive oil in a large bowl.

Mince the dried herbs using a mortar and pestle. Add the the bowl with the chanterelles and olive oil, and toss to coat.

Spread the chanterelles out evenly on a baking sheet with a parchment paper lining. Season with salt and pepper.

Bake for 20 minutes, turning once in the middle. Serve hot as a side to your favourite meat or as an appetizer with red wine.

Dessert: Mulberry-Huckleberry Loaf

Chapter 11:

Additional Resources

In this final chapter, you'll find directions to additional resources such as websites, groups, and books that can help you along on your foraging journey.

General Pacific Northwest

NorthernBushcraft.com: A comprehensive site with listing of edible plant species by state in the Pacific Northwest.

PNWFishandForage.com: An excellent website for beginners, with articles on identifying, harvesting, and preparing foraged foods found in the Pacific Northwest.

PNW Foraging and Wild Edibles: Facebook group for people of all walks of life and skill levels who enjoy foraging in the Pacific Northwest. Users post discussions, news, tips, photos, recipes, and more.

Washington

Foraging Washington: Finding, Identifying, and Preparing Wild Foods in Oregon by Christopher Nyerges: A comprehensive book on foraging in Washington and how to identify the state's edible plants.

WashingtonsLastFrontier.com: A homesteading website focused on Washington state with extensive guides to foraging for plants and mushrooms.

Oregon

Foraging Oregon Facebook Group: An active online community for foragers in Oregon state.

Foraging Oregon: Finding, Identifying, and Preparing Wild Foods in Oregon by Christopher Nyerges: A comprehensive book on foraging in Oregon and how to identify the state's edible plants.

TravelOregon.com: A tourism website for Oregon State which includes a useful guide on local edible mushrooms.

Idaho

The Southern Idaho Mycological Organization: An organization offering mushroom foraging tours and classes in the state.

VisitMcCall.org: An official tourism website of the McCall region, where foraging is legal and wild edible plants are abundant. The website includes a guide to harvesting some wild plants found in the region.

FungalForager.com: A website offering information on mushroom foraging in Idaho.

Conclusion

Fig 39. A landscape in Idaho. From: Unsplash, by Fudo Jahic, 2019. https://unsplash.com/photos/gx93r8jATgo Copyright Fudo Jahic, 2019.

At last, you're ready to start out on your foraging journey. Not only have you become familiar with some of the edible (and non-edible) plants in the beautiful Pacific Northwest, you've also learned some of the many uses for them, from medicinal infusions and tinctures, flavorful recipes, and delicious jams, jellies, preserves, and pickles. You've also learned some additional important information, such as what to pack for a foraging expedition, the right tools for the job, and how to make your harvests last until you're ready to eat them. Finally, you've learned how to forage safely and legally by navigating encounters with wildlife, avoiding protected areas and private property, being aware of where plants may be contaminated, and never harvesting something that you have not identified for certain.

People have been foraging since prehistoric times. Full of delicious edible plants and useful medicinal herbs, the natural world has never let us down with it's endless bounty. When foraging, the most important thing to remember after keeping yourself safe is that it's also important to preserve the environment. We can do this by never harvesting more than we need and never letting our harvests go to waste, using the guides to preserving food included in this manual. Furthermore, only taking ⅕ (at most) of the plants available, and leaving lone plants alone, ensures that we will not strip a particular area of an important keystone species. The great thing about foraging is that if you want more, you can always go out again!

If we all take responsibility, and with a bit of luck, the breathtaking hills, coastlines, and forests of the Pacific Northwest will remain just as pristine for future generations to enjoy. We wish you best of luck on your foraging journey, and hope you come back safe with a delicious harvest to enjoy!

Thank you for choosing us!

Thank you for selecting our book, out of the wide range of options available to you. With so many books on the same topic, we're very appreciative that you decided to choose ours and read through to the end!

If you enjoyed our book, we'd like to ask you to consider posting a review on the Amazon Platform. Reviews are essential to independent authors like us in order to continue bringing you this great content! We value your feedback and would love to hear what you think.

We thank you again for choosing our book, and we look forward to hearing from you!

References

Adan, E. (2015, March 6). *A guide to foraging safety: 7 tips.* Aquaberry Bliss. https://aquaberrybliss.com/2015/03/06/a-guide-to-foraging-safety-7-tips/

Awkward Botany. (2017, May 31). *Poisonous plants: Buttercups.* Awkward Botany. https://awkwardbotany.com/2017/05/31/poisonous-plants-buttercups/

Blasbalg, R. (2021, July 12). *How to use mulberry medicinally.* The Lost Herbs. https://thelostherbs.com/how-to-use-mulberry-medicinally/

Chestnut School of Herbal Medicine. (2019, August 21). *Goldenrod: Medicinal uses & benefits.* Chestnut School of Herbal Medicine. https://chestnutherbs.com/medicinal-uses-and-benefits-of-goldenrod/

Covington, L. (2020). *Stop wasting herbs—here are the best ways to dry them.* The Spruce Eats. https://www.thespruceeats.com/harvesting-and-drying-leafy-herbs-1327541

Culver, B. (2020, June 12). *Foraging with kids: 5 easy-to-find wild edibles.* An off Grid Life. https://www.anoffgridlife.com/foraging-with-kids/

Culver, B. (2021a, May 22). *How to use a fermenting crock*. An Off Grid Life. https://www.anoffgridlife.com/how-to-use-a-fermenting-crock/

Culver, B. (2021b, June 5). *Pickling for beginners: How to get started*. An Off Grid Life. https://www.anoffgridlife.com/pickling-for-beginners-how-to-get-started/

Daw, S. (2021). *Pacific poison oak*. www.nps.gov. https://www.nps.gov/articles/000/pacific-poison-oak.htm

Dyer, M. H. (2018, April 4). *What is Indian pipe plant*. Gardening Know How. https://www.gardeningknowhow.com/ornamental/fungus-lichen/indian-pipe-fungus.htm

Dyer, M. H. (2020). *Baneberry plant information: What are red or white baneberry plants*. Gardening Know How. https://www.gardeningknowhow.com/ornamental/shrubs/baneberry/baneberry-plant-information.htm

Dyer, M. H. (2021). *Horsetails*. Gardeningknowhow.com. https://www.gardeningknowhow.com/edible/herbs/horsetail/harvesting-horsetail-herbs.htm

Eckberg, J., Hopwood, J., & Lee-Mäder, E. (2016). *Collecting and using your own wildflower seed to expand pollinator habitat on farms*. https://backyardhabitats.org/wp-content/uploads/2019/10/Collecting-Your-Own-Wildflower-Seeds.pdf

Edible Wild Food. (2021a). *Apricot jelly identification: Pictures, habitat, season & spore print | Guepinia helvelloides.* Ediblewildfood.com. https://www.ediblewildfood.com/apricot-jelly.aspx

Edible Wild Food. (2021b). *Cattail: Pictures, flowers, leaves & identification | Typha latifolia.* Www.ediblewildfood.com. https://www.ediblewildfood.com/cattail.aspx

Edible Wild Food. (2021c). *Horsetail: Pictures, flowers, leaves & identification | Equisetum arvense.* Ediblewildfood.com. https://www.ediblewildfood.com/horsetail.aspx

EdibleWildFood.com. (2021). *Russian olive: Identification, leaves, bark & habitat.* Ediblewildfood.com. https://www.ediblewildfood.com/russian-olive.aspx

Emergency Essentials. (2014). *How to identify poisonous plants.* Be Prepared - Emergency Essentials. https://beprepared.com/blogs/articles/how-to-identify-poisonous-plants

First Nature. (2021). *Lycoperdon perlatum, common puffball, identification.* First-Nature.com. https://www.first-nature.com/fungi/lycoperdon-perlatum.php

Food Network Magazine. (2021). *How to make preserves: Jam, jelly, compote, salsa and more.* Food Com.

https://www.foodnetwork.com/recipes/photos/how-to-preserve

Forager's Harvest. (2013). *Fern fiddleheads the succulent stalks of spring.*
https://www.foragersharvest.com/uploads/9/2/1/2/92123698/fern_fiddleheads.pdf

Foster, K. (2016). *What's the difference between pickling and fermenting?* Kitchn.
https://www.thekitchn.com/whats-the-difference-between-pickling-and-fermenting-229536

Good Life Revival. (2017). *How to identify chickweed.* Good Life Revival.
https://thegoodliferevival.com/blog/chickweed

Grant, A. (2021). *Edible parts of cattails.* Gardeningknowhow.com.
https://www.gardeningknowhow.com/ornamental/water-plants/cattails/edible-parts-of-cattail.htm

Harbour, S. (2020, August 14). *Easy ways to get started canning right now.* An Off Grid Life.
https://www.anoffgridlife.com/get-started-canning/

Health Benefits Times. (2019, October 20). *Miner's lettuce facts and health benefits.* HealthBenefitsTimes.com.
https://www.healthbenefitstimes.com/miners-lettuce/

Heath, A. (2021, August 9). *All about deadly galerina | identify, toxicity & treatments.* Helping & Useful Stories. https://blog.inspireuplift.com/galerina-marginata/

Herbal Academy. (2014, July 3). *Yarrow as a natural remedy for fever and flu.* Herbal Academy. https://theherbalacademy.com/yarrow-as-a-natural-remedy-for-fever-and-flu/

Hunting and Fishing BC. (2021). *Edible wild mushrooms.* Rivermen Rod and Gun Club. http://www.rivermenrodandgunclub.com/edible-wild-mushrooms.html

King County. (2019). *Poison-hemlock identification and control: Conium maculatum - King County.* Kingcounty.gov. https://kingcounty.gov/services/environment/animals-and-plants/noxious-weeds/weed-identification/poison-hemlock.aspx

Larum, D. (2021). *Yarrow plant uses - what are the benefits of yarrow?* Www.gardeningknowhow.com. https://www.gardeningknowhow.com/edible/herbs/yarrow/yarrow-plant-uses-and-benefits.htm

Mariott, M. (2010). *Medicinal plants of the north cascades specific to the Environmental Learning Center natural history project and presentation.* https://ncascades.org/discover/north-cascades-ecosystem/files/Medicinal%20Plants%20of%20the%20%20North%20Cascades.pdf

McCall Idaho, Let's Go! (2021). *Foraging.* McCall Idaho, Let's Go! https://visitmccall.org/things-to-do/activity/foraging/

Medical Dictionary. (2021). *Nervine.* The Free Dictionary. https://medical-dictionary.thefreedictionary.com/nervine

Medicinal Herbs. (2021). *Indian pipe - Monotropa uniflora.* Naturalmedicinalherbs.net. http://www.naturalmedicinalherbs.net/herbs/m/monotropa-uniflora=indian-pipe.php

Meredith, L. (2019a). *How to dry mushrooms in your oven.* The Spruce Eats. https://www.thespruceeats.com/how-to-dry-mushrooms-oven-method-1327547

Meredith, L. (2019b). *The right way to sterilize canning jars.* The Spruce Eats. https://www.thespruceeats.com/how-to-sterilize-canning-jars-1327595

Meredith, L. (2020). *How to perform pressure canning.* The Spruce Eats. https://www.thespruceeats.com/pressure-canning-step-by-step-guide-1327465

Moore, D. (2020, July 23). *Destroying angel mushrooms.* Mushroom KnowHow. https://www.mushroomknowhow.com/destroying-angel-mushrooms/

Moutain Rose Herbs. (2014). *Making herbal jam & jelly!* Mountainroseherbs.com.

https://blog.mountainroseherbs.com/making-herbal-jelly-superfood-recipe

Mushrooms, M. (2019). *How to properly dry or dehydrate mushrooms.* www.montereymushrooms.com. https://www.montereymushrooms.com/blog/how-to-properly-dry-or-dehydrate-mushrooms

Natural Medicinal Herbs. (2021). *Medicinal herbs: Mountain dandelion - agoseris glauca.* Naturalmedicinalherbs.net. http://naturalmedicinalherbs.net/herbs/a/agoseris-glauca=mountain-dandelion.php

Nebraska Advocates. (2021). *Most dangerous animals in the Pacific Northwest.* www.nebraskaadvocates.com. https://www.nebraskaadvocates.com/state/the-most-dangerous-animals-in-the-pacific-northwest/

Ng, D. (2018). *Thistle identification.* Hunker. https://www.hunker.com/12284915/thistle-identification

Noivelle, A. (2019, April 25). *An herbalist's guide to using self heal.* Indie Herbalist. https://blog.indieherbalist.com/an-herbalists-guide-to-using-self-heal/

Northern Bushcraft. (2021). *Knotweed (Polygonum spp.) in British Columbia.* Www.northernbushcraft.com. https://www.northernbushcraft.com/topic.php?name=knotweed®ion=pnw&ctgy=edible_plants

Northern Bushcraft. (2021e). *Wild edible mushrooms of the Pacific Northwest.* Northernbushcraft.com. https://northernbushcraft.com/mushrooms/

Northern Bushcraft. (2021f). *Wild edible plants of the Pacific Northwest.* Www.northernbushcraft.com. https://www.northernbushcraft.com/plants/

Nwadike, L. (2015). *Safely fermenting food at home extension food safety fact sheet.* https://nifa.usda.gov/sites/default/files/resource/ Safely%20Fermenting%20Food%20at%20Home% 20508.pdf

Nyerges, C. (2016). *Foraging Oregon: Finding, identifying, and preparing edible wild foods in Oregon (foraging series).* Falcon Field Guides.

Oregon Fish and Wildlife Office. (2020). *Gentner's fritillary.* www.fws.gov. https://www.fws.gov/oregonfwo/articles.cfm?id= 149489432

Painter, T. (2021). *The best time of year to harvest watercress.* Home Guides | SF Gate. https://homeguides.sfgate.com/time-year-harvest-watercress-68110.html

Pearce, K. (2021). *The edible and medicinal plants of the Pacific Northwest.* INaturalist. https://www.inaturalist.org/guides/10285

Pexels. (2021). *Photo by Roman Pohorecki on Pexels*. Pexels. https://www.pexels.com/photo/brown-mushroom-16706/

Pilot, T. (2021, August 10). *Toxic berries in the Pacific Northwest*. Trip Pilot. https://www.trippilot.net/post/toxic-berries-in-the-pacific-northwest

Pixabay. (2013). *Photo by ArtTower on Pixabay*. Pixabay. https://pixabay.com/photos/horsetail-scouring-rush-plants-123013/

Pixabay. (2013a). *Photo by James Demers on Pixabay*. Pixabay. https://pixabay.com/photos/poison-ivy-toxicodendron-radicans-195123/

Pixabay. (2013b). *Photo by NatureFriend on Pixabay*. Pixabay. https://pixabay.com/photos/mushrooms-mushroom-tree-trunk-295823/

Pixabay. (2014a). *Photo by alsen on Pixabay*. Pixabay. https://pixabay.com/photos/watercress-blossom-bloom-spring-333746/

Pixabay. (2014b). *Photo by WikimediaImages on Pixabay*. Pixabay. https://pixabay.com/photos/beargrass-white-flower-wild-flower-1282962/

Pixabay. (2015). *Photo by Ellen26 on Pixabay*. Pixabay. https://pixabay.com/photos/beargrass-white-flower-wild-flower-1282962/

Pixabay. (2016). *Photo by kfalk on Pixabay.* Pixabay. https://pixabay.com/photos/mushroom-spongy-cauliflower-mushroom-1784177/

Pixabay. (2017). *Photo by HOerwin56 on Pixabay.* Pixabay. https://pixabay.com/photos/knotweed-shrub-plant-2699120/

Pixabay. (2017a). *Photo by Goumbik on Pixabay.* Pixabay. https://pixabay.com/photos/hand-berry-nature-bush-natural-2717117/

Pixabay. (2017b). *Photo by Perkons on Pixabay.* Pixabay. https://pixabay.com/photos/sulphur-mushroom-2362179/

Pixabay. (2019a). *Photo by brosimoff on Pixabay.* Pixabay. https://pixabay.com/photos/ghost-pipes-monotropa-uniflora-plant-5756786/

Pixabay. (2019b). *Photo by kleigweg1 on Pixabay.* Pixabay. https://pixabay.com/photos/fungi-forrest-nature-decorative-4501878/

Pixabay. (2019c). *Photo by Mike Goad on Pixabay.* Pixabay. https://pixabay.com/photos/red-baneberries-bane-berries-3963764/

Pixabay. (2020a). *Photo by Akuptsova on Pixabay.* Pixabay. https://pixabay.com/photos/plantain-medicinal-plants-meadow-6198631/

Pixabay. (2020b). *Photo by JACKLOU-DL on Pixabay.* Pixabay. https://pixabay.com/photos/plant-bush-stems-petals-hemlock-5502057/

Pixabay. (2021). *Photo by Lakeblog on Pixabay.* Pixabay. https://pixabay.com/photos/salmonberries-unripe-6473360/

Pixabay. (2021a). *Photo by artellliii72 on Pixabay.* Pixabay. https://pixabay.com/photos/morels-mushrooms-spring-nature-6241791/

Pixabay. (2021b). *Photo by ulleo on Pixabay.* Pixabay. https://pixabay.com/photos/fern-fiddlehead-plant-spring-6258134/

Plants for a Future. (2021). *Glaux maritima black saltwort, sea milkwort.* Pfaf.org. https://pfaf.org/User/Plant.aspx?LatinName=Glaux+maritima

Practical Self Reliance. (2019, June 11). *Foraging miner's lettuce.* Practical Self Reliance. https://practicalselfreliance.com/foraging-miners-lettuce/

Project Noah. (2021). *Poisonous plants of the Pacific Northwest.* Project Noah. https://www.projectnoah.org/missions/16931698

Rossi, M. (2018). *10 guidelines for ethical foraging.* www.finedininglovers.com.

https://www.finedininglovers.com/article/10-guidelines-ethical-foraging

Salomon.com. (2021). *How to choose your hiking backpack.* Salomon. https://www.salomon.com/en-us/outdoor/outdoor-advice/how-choose-your-hiking-backpack

Shaw, H. (2013, July 29). *Foraging for gooseberries - how to identify, gather and eat gooseberries.* Hunter Angler Gardener Cook. https://honest-food.net/wild-gooseberries-edible/

Shock, L. (2021). *Devils club.* Nativeplantsociety.org. http://www.nativeplantsociety.org/devils-club

Spotten, S. (2012, June 7). *Identifying and using pineapple weed.* Midwest Permaculture. https://midwestpermaculture.com/2012/06/identifying-and-using-pineapple-weed-3/

Stevens, M., & Darris, D. (2000). *Plant guide: Salmonberry (Rubus spectabilis).* https://www.nrcs.usda.gov/Internet/FSE_PLANT MATERIALS/publications/orpmcpg10952.pdf

Stewart, G. (2020, May 2). *How to harvest stinging nettle for use in everyday cooking.* GettyStewart.com. https://www.gettystewart.com/how-to-harvest-dry-freeze-use-stinging-nettle/

Sturluson, T. (2017, April 3). *Ethical foraging – do's and don'ts.* The Herbal Resource. https://www.herbal-supplement-resource.com/ethical-foraging/

SunnySports.com. (2018, June 12). *Pacific Northwest poisonous mushrooms: 5 species to avoid.* Sunny Sports Blog. https://www.sunnysports.com/blog/5-mushrooms-avoid-pacific-northwest/

Taste of Home Editors. (2019, June 7). *How to make perfect pickles.* Taste of Home. https://www.tasteofhome.com/article/how-to-make-pickles/

The FunGal Forager. (2018, November 8). *Explore Idaho's edible mushrooms and wild plants.* The FunGal Forager. https://fungalforager.com/

The Great Morel. (2021). *False morels.* The Great Morel. https://www.thegreatmorel.com/false-morels/

The Homestead Garden. (2011, September 19). *Medicinal uses of yarrow.* The Homestead Garden. https://www.thehomesteadgarden.com/medicinal-uses-of-yarrow/

The Primal Desire. (2020). *Stuffed morel mushrooms recipe.* Yummly.com. https://www.yummly.com/recipe/Stuffed-Morel-Mushrooms-2453931?prm-v1#directions

The Southern Idaho Mycological Organization. (2021). *Home*. Southern Idaho Mycological Association. https://idahomushroomclub.org/

The Ultimate Mushroom Guide. (2021). *Conocybe tenera*. Ultimate Mushroom Library. https://ultimate-mushroom.com/poisonous/194-conocybe-tenera.html

Timberlake, S. (2020). *7 steps to safe home canning*. The Spruce Eats. https://www.thespruceeats.com/guide-to-water-bath-canning-1327461

TravelOregon.com. (2021, September 27). *Beginner's guide to mushroom foraging in Oregon*. Travel Oregon. https://traveloregon.com/plan-your-trip/guides-tours/tours-guided-trips/beginners-guide-to-mushroom-foraging-in-oregon/

Turf Tips. (2021). *Broadleaf plantain. Turfgrass Science at Purdue University*. https://turf.purdue.edu/broadleaf-plantain/

Turner Photographics. (2021). *Achillea millefolium | common yarrow | wildflowers of the Pacific Northwest*. Www.pnwflowers.com. https://www.pnwflowers.com/flower/achillea-millefolium

Turner, M. (2021a). *Achillea millefolium | common yarrow*. www.pnwflowers.com. https://www.pnwflowers.com/flower/achillea-millefolium

Turner, M. (2021b). *Solanum dulcamara | bittersweet nightshade.* Pnwflowers.com. https://www.pnwflowers.com/flower/solanum-dulcamara

TyrantFarms. (2020, August 27). *Cauliflower mushrooms: How to find, ID, and eat (with quiche recipe!).* Tyrant Farms. https://www.tyrantfarms.com/cauliflower-mushrooms-how-to-find-id-and-eat-with-quiche-recipe/

U.S. Forest Service. (2021). *Pacific Northwest region rare plant profiles.* www.fs.fed.us. https://www.fs.fed.us/wildflowers/Rare_Plants/profiles/pacificnorthwest.shtml

US Fish and Wildlife Service. (2021). *Species fact sheet golden paintbrush Castilleja levisecta.* https://www.fws.gov/wafwo/species/Fact%20sheets/GPaintbrush_factsheet.pdf

UVM Medical Center. (2017, September 8). *Poisonous plants: What to do if you touch, eat, or burn a harmful plant.* UVM Medical Center Blog. https://medcenterblog.uvmhealth.org/wellness/poisonous-plants-health-safety/

United States Department of Agriculture. (2015). *Complete guide to principles of home canning.* https://nchfp.uga.edu/publications/usda/GUIDE01_HomeCan_rev0715.pdf

University of California. (2021). *Common knotweed (prostrate knotweed).* Ipm.ucanr.edu. http://ipm.ucanr.edu/PMG/WEEDS/common_k notweed.html

University of Maryland Extension. (2021). *How to identify poison ivy.* Extension.umd.edu. https://extension.umd.edu/resource/how-identify-poison-ivy

UnrulyGardening.com. (2021, September 2). *Foraging & using self heal.* Unruly Gardening. https://unrulygardening.com/foraging-using-self-heal/

Unsplash. (2017). *Photo by S&B Vonlanthen on Unsplash.* Unsplash.com. https://unsplash.com/photos/D75_5tWZDQ4

Unsplash. (2018). *Photo by Marcus Wallis on Unsplash.* Unsplash.com. https://unsplash.com/photos/MTeZ5FmCGCU

Unsplash. (2018a). *Photo by Dave Hoefler on Unsplash.* Unsplash.com. https://unsplash.com/photos/rcE3_D-u2NE

Unsplash. (2018b). *Photo by Paul Morley on Unsplash.* Unsplash.com. https://unsplash.com/photos/DrYqMhk53dY

Unsplash. (2019a). *Photo by Alice Pasqual on Unsplash.* Unsplash.com. https://unsplash.com/photos/xdD-x2Y2SPI

Unsplash. (2019a). *Photo by James Whitney on Unsplash.* Unsplash.com. https://unsplash.com/photos/Z_JF_BjNbZY

Unsplash. (2019b). *Photo by Fudo Jahic on Unsplash.* Unsplash.com. https://unsplash.com/photos/gx93r8jATgo

Unsplash. (2019b). *Photo by Jeffrey Hamilton on Unsplash.* Unsplash.com. https://unsplash.com/photos/JMuJfLVWtN4

Unsplash. (2020). *Photo by Olli Kilpi on Unsplash.* Unsplash.com. https://unsplash.com/photos/PRWPNWnS4eU

Unsplash. (2020a). *Photo by Alistair MacRobert on Unsplash.* Unsplash.com. https://unsplash.com/photos/vjdu7KWzKM0

Unsplash. (2020b). *Photo by Denny Müller on Unsplash.* Unsplash.com. https://unsplash.com/photos/WVRGWpbn37Y

Unsplash. (2020c). *Photo by Friderike on Unsplash.* Unsplash.com. https://unsplash.com/photos/IyulfxSdgWE

Unsplash. (2020d). *Photo by John Thomas on Unsplash.* Unsplash.com. https://unsplash.com/photos/FdKDKLoSa0M

Unsplash. (2020e). *Photo by Matt Seymour on Unsplash.* Unsplash.com. https://unsplash.com/photos/Awaf_6vEdtI

Unsplash. (2021). *Photo by Timothy Dykes on Unsplash.* Unsplash.com. https://unsplash.com/photos/pwE2OExLYc0

Unsplash. (2021a). *Photo by Annie Spratt on Unsplash.* Unsplash.com. https://unsplash.com/photos/FUmGvzRgrmM

Unsplash. (2021b). *Photo by Ray Harrington on Unsplash.* Unsplash.com. https://unsplash.com/photos/MBeBLtuHOF0

Washington State University. (2021). *Russian olive - Elaeagnus angustifolia.* Pnwplants.wsu.edu. http://pnwplants.wsu.edu/PlantDisplay.aspx?PlantID=567

Washington State University. (2021). *Selected poisonous plants of the Pacific Northwest.* Animal Agriculture. https://extension.wsu.edu/animalag/content/selected-poisonous-plants-of-the-pacific-northwest/

Watson, M. (2021). *What are oyster mushrooms?* The Spruce Eats. https://www.thespruceeats.com/what-are-oyster-mushrooms-4172003

WebMD. (2019). Watercress: *Uses, side effects, interactions, dosage, and warning.* Webmd.com. https://www.webmd.com/vitamins/ai/ingredient mono-346/watercress

Whitehead, P., & Starzomski, B. (2014). *Sea milkwort.* Biodiversity of the Central Coast. https://www.centralcoastbiodiversity.org/sea-milkwort-bull-glaux-maritima.html

Winger, J. (2019, September 24). *How to use a fermenting crock.* The Prairie Homestead. https://www.theprairiehomestead.com/2019/09/how-to-use-a-fermenting-crock.html

York CCD. (2019). *American holly.* Identification Pages for Tree Species. https://www.yorkccd.org/wp-content/uploads/2019/12/Identification-pages-for-tree-species.pdf

Young, D. (2017, March 20). *Ethical foraging 101: What you need to know.* LearningHerbs. Https://learningherbs.com/skills/foraging/